# Supporting Students in a Time
## of Core Standards

# Supporting Students in a Time of Core Standards

English Language Arts, Grades 6–8

Tonya Perry
*University of Alabama at Birmingham*

with
Rebecca Manery
*The University of Michigan*

National Council of Teachers of English
1111 W. Kenyon Road, Urbana, Illinois 61801-1096

*Manuscript Editor:* THERESA KAY
*Staff Editor:* BONNY GRAHAM
*Interior Design:* JENNY JENSEN GREENLEAF
*Cover Design:* PAT MAYER
*Cover Background:* ISTOCKPHOTO.COM/ARTIOM MUHACIOV

NCTE Stock Number: 49423

**Library of Congress Cataloging-in-Publication Data**

Perry, Tonya.
  Supporting students in a time of core standards : English language arts, grades 6–8 / Tonya Perry with Rebecca Manery.
       p. cm.
  Includes bibliographical references.
  ISBN 978-0-8141-4942-3 ((pbk))
  1. Language arts (Middle school)--Standards--United States. 2. Language arts (Middle school)--Curricula--United States. 3. Education--Standards--United States. 4. Effective teaching--United States. I. Manery, Rebecca. II. Title
CURR LB1631.P42 2011
    428.0071'2--dc23
                                                                    2011035735

# Contents

# I

# Observing the CCSS

# ⊚ Introduction

Not long ago I was driving a van filled with middle school soccer players and heard a voice from the back say, "I hate, I hate, I hate the MEAP." (The MEAP is Michigan's state test of math and English language arts [ELA].) I recognized the voice as that of a friend of my daughter, a good student, diligent in every way. Her class had just spent a month preparing for and then taking the MEAP, and she was feeling frustrated by the time spent and anxious about her performance.

That plaintive voice reminded me of concerns I've heard expressed about the latest chapter in the standards movement. The appearance of the Common Core State Standards (CCSS) has aroused a variety of responses, some of them filled with anxiety and resentment. It's easy to get worried about issues of alignment, curricular shifts, and new forms of assessment. And it's frustrating, after carefully developing state ELA standards, to have to put them aside in favor of the CCSS. As one teacher put it, "The CCSS are less detailed than the standards they are replacing." Another lamented, "How are teachers supposed to have time to rewrite curriculum and realign lessons to CCSS now that the state has taken away our meeting times?"

Yet, responses to the CCSS have also been positive. Some teachers have said that the grade-specific standards are helpful because they provide useful details about learning goals for students. Others have noted that the CCSS can help them address the needs of transient students because teachers in different schools will be addressing similar learning goals. Still others have commented that the CCSS can provide a lens through which they can examine their own teaching practices. As one teacher put it, "Looking at the standards made me realize that I wasn't giving much attention to oral language." Another said, "I think they provide more opportunities for higher-order thinking and an authentic application of the content we teach."

Regardless of teacher responses, the CCSS are now part of the educational landscape. But these standards do not replace the principles that guide good teaching. Some things remain constant regardless of new mandates. One such principle is that teachers think first of their students, trying to understand their learning needs, developing effective ways to meet those needs, and continually affirming that the needs are being met. This book, like all four volumes in this series, is written with and by teachers who remain deeply committed to their students and their literacy learning. It is a book addressed to teachers like you. You may be an experienced teacher who has established ways of fostering literacy learning or you may be a relative newcomer to the classroom who is looking for ideas and strategies, but that you are holding this book in your hands says that you put students at the center of your teaching.

No one knows as much about your students as you do. You understand the community that surrounds the school and helps to shape their life experiences. You have some information about their families and may even know their parents or guardians personally. You can tell when they are having difficulty and when they are feeling successful. You have watched their body language, scanned their faces, listened to their voices, and read enough of their writing to have some ideas about what matters to them. Your knowledge about your students guides the instructional choices you make, and it shapes your response to any mandate, including the CCSS.

Your knowledge about students is probably connected to your knowledge of assessment. You know the importance of finding out what students have learned and what they still need to learn. You probably already know about the importance of authentic assessment, measures of learning that are connected with work students can be expected to do outside of class as well as in it. No doubt you use formative assessment, measures of learning that give students feedback rather than grades and help you know what they still need to learn. For example, you probably make sure that students respond to one another's written drafts as they develop a finished piece of writing. You may have individual conferences with student writers or offer marginal comments and suggestions on their drafts. Or perhaps you meet individually with students to hear them read aloud or tell you about what they have been reading. Whatever type of formative assessment you use, you probably use it to guide the decisions you make about teaching.

You may have read or heard about the Principles for Learning adopted by NCTE and other subject-matter associations, principles that position literacy at the heart of learning in all subjects, describe learning as social, affirm the value of learning about learning, urge the importance of assessing progress, emphasize new media, and see learning in a global context. These principles, like others articulated by NCTE, provide a North Star to guide instruction regardless of specific mandates, and you probably recognize that teaching based on such principles will foster student achievement, including achievement of the CCSS.

Because you are concerned about the learning of *all* of your students, you probably try to find ways to affirm the wide variety of racial, ethnic, socioeconomic, and religious backgrounds that students bring into the classroom. No doubt you are interested in taking multiple approaches to reading, writing, speaking, and listening so that you can engage as many students as possible. Taking this stance convinces you that continual growth and innovation are essential to student achievement, especially when new standards are being introduced.

This book is designed to support you in meeting the challenges posed by the CCSS. It stands on the principle that standards do not mean standardization or a one-size-fits-all approach to teaching. It assumes that inspirational teaching—teaching that engages students as critical problem solvers who embrace multiple ways of representing knowledge—can address standards most effectively. It celebrates new visions of innovation and the renewal of long-held visions that may have become buried in the midst of day-to-day obligations. It reinforces a focus on student learning by demonstrating ways of addressing these standards while also adhering to NCTE principles of effective teaching. It does this by, first, examining the CCSS to identify key features and address some of the most common questions they raise. The second section of this book moves into the classrooms of individual teachers, offering snapshots of instruction and showing how teachers developed their practices across time. These classroom snapshots demonstrate ways to address learning goals included in the CCSS while simultaneously adhering to principles of good teaching articulated by NCTE. In addition to narratives of teaching, this section includes charts that show, quickly, how principles and standards can be aligned. Finally, this section offers suggestions for professional development, both for individuals and for teachers who participate in communities of practice. Thanks to NCTE's online resources, you can join in a community of practice that extends across local and state boundaries, enabling you to share ideas and strategies with colleagues from many parts of the country. Embedded throughout this section are student work samples and many other artifacts, and NCTE's online resources include many more materials, from which you can draw and to which you can contribute. The final section of this book recognizes that effective change requires long-term planning as well as collaboration among colleagues, and it offers strategies and materials for planning units of study articulating grade-level expectations and mapping yearlong instruction.

Voices in the back of your mind, like the "I hate, I hate" voice in the back of my van, may continue to express frustrations and anxieties about the CCSS, but I am confident that the teachers you will meet in this book along with the ideas and strategies offered will reinforce your view of yourself as a professional educator charged with making decisions about strategies and curriculum to advance the learning of your students.

Anne Ruggles Gere
Series Editor

# Demystifying the Common Core State Standards

As an eighth-grade teacher, I know that my students are headed for high school, so having a document that shows me where the students have been and where they should be ready to perform when they get to the next level is helpful. Another consideration is that these standards outline literacy goals for other subject areas as well. This underscores that teaching literacy skills is not just the job of English language arts teachers, but the responsibility of every subject-area teacher. I think it will facilitate cross-curricular planning and improve teaching across the board. Most importantly, I can see the CCSS helping me by giving me a gauge on my own teaching to make sure I am adequately preparing my students for lifelong learning and literacy. The students are the focus.

—MARY JAMES, MIDDLE SCHOOL TEACHER

Putting students at the center means thinking first about the kinds of learning experiences we want them to have, and since forty-plus states have adopted the Common Core State Standards (CCSS), many teachers will need to think about student learning in light of these standards. First, though, it will be helpful to understand where these standards came from and what they actually say.

The CCSS are part of a long-term movement toward greater accountability in education that stretches back to the early 1990s. In this line of thinking, accountability focuses on student achievement rather than, say, time spent in classrooms or materials used, and standards like the ones developed by states beginning in the 1990s have been used to indicate what students should achieve. Because of this emphasis, standards are often equated with educational transformation, as in "standards-based school reform." Proponents of standards-based reform have differing views of how standards should be used. Some assume that standards can lead to investments and curricular changes that will improve schools, while others see them as linked to testing that has little to do with allocating resources that will change schools for the better. This book operates from the assumption that ELA teachers can use standards as a lens through which they can

**Web 1.1**
Throughout this volume, you will find links, reproducibles, interactive opportunities, and other online resources indicated by this icon. Go online to www.ncte.org/books/supp-students-6-8 to take advantage of these materials.

examine and improve the *what* and *how* of instruction, and the vignettes in Section II demonstrate how teachers are doing this.

The CCSS for English Language Arts and Mathematics, then, are the latest in a series of standards-based school reform initiatives. They were coordinated by the National Governors Association Center for Best Practices (NGA Center) and the Council of Chief State School Officers (CCSSO) to prepare US students for both college and the workplace. This partnership of state governors and state school superintendents worked with Achieve Inc., an education reform organization founded in 1996 and based in Washington, DC, to develop the CCSS. Funding for their work was provided by the Bill and Melinda Gates Foundation, the Charles Steward Mott Foundation, and other private groups. Each state decided whether to adopt the CCSS, and the US Department of Education created an incentive by linking adoption of the CCSS to Race to the Top (RTT), requiring states that applied for RTT funds to adopt the CCSS. When the CCSS were released in June of 2010, more than forty states had already agreed to adopt them.

In the states that have formally adopted them, the CCSS will replace state standards. States may add 15 percent, which means that some elements of state standards could be preserved or new standards could be developed. The full text of the ELA standards, along with other explanatory materials, is available online at http://www .corestandards.org/the-standards/english-language-arts-standards.

In September of 2010, two consortia of states, the Partnership for the Assessment of Readiness for College and Careers (PARCC) and the SMARTER Balanced Assessment Consortium, were funded—also with RTT monies—to develop assessments to accompany the CCSS, and these assessments are scheduled for implementation in 2014. At this point it is impossible to know precisely what the assessments will include, but preliminary documents indicate that formative assessment may play a role, that computers may be involved in both administration and scoring, and that some parts of the assessment, such as writing, may occur over multiple days.

**Web 1.2**

For updates on the development of CCSS assessments, check online.

### I don't have time to read through the entire CCSS document, so can you give me a quick summary?

The ELA standards for grades 6–12 address four basic strands for ELA: reading, writing, speaking and listening, and language. Although each is presented separately, the introduction to the CCSS in English Language Arts advocates for an integrated model of literacy in which all four dimensions are interwoven. In addition, the CCSS for grades 6–12 include standards for history/social studies and science and technical subjects, which have reading and writing strands. Each strand has overarching Anchor

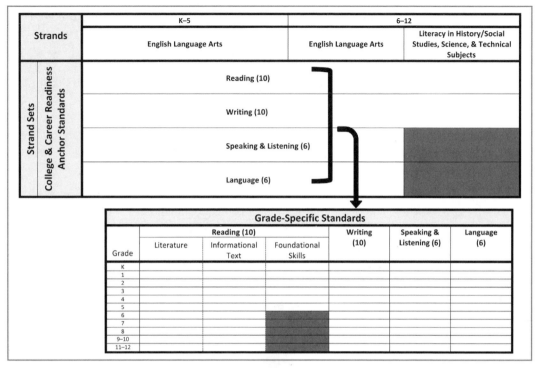

| Strands | K–5 | | 6–12 | |
|---|---|---|---|---|
| | English Language Arts | | English Language Arts | Literacy in History/Social Studies, Science, & Technical Subjects |

**Strand Sets** — **College & Career Readiness Anchor Standards**

- Reading (10)
- Writing (10)
- Speaking & Listening (6)
- Language (6)

**Grade-Specific Standards**

| Grade | Reading (10) | | | Writing (10) | Speaking & Listening (6) | Language (6) |
|---|---|---|---|---|---|---|
| | Literature | Informational Text | Foundational Skills | | | |
| K | | | | | | |
| 1 | | | | | | |
| 2 | | | | | | |
| 3 | | | | | | |
| 4 | | | | | | |
| 5 | | | | | | |
| 6 | | | | | | |
| 7 | | | | | | |
| 8 | | | | | | |
| 9–10 | | | | | | |
| 11–12 | | | | | | |

**FIGURE 1.1:** Structural relationships of the CCSS.

Standards, which are translated into grade-specific standards. Figure 1.1 shows the structural relationship of the two.

The content of the two is similarly linked. For example, the 6–12 Anchor Standards for writing include the category "text types and purposes," and one of the Anchor Standards in this category reads, "write arguments to support claims in an analysis of substantive topics or texts, using valid reasoning and relevant and sufficient evidence." One of the three sixth-grade standards that addresses this Anchor Standard includes the following:

- Write arguments to support claims with clear reasons and relevant evidence.
- Introduce claim(s) and organize the reasons and evidence clearly.
- Support claim(s) with clear reasons and relevant evidence, using credible sources and demonstrating an understanding of the topic or text.

- Use words, phrases, and clauses to clarify the relationships among claim(s) and reasons.

- Establish and maintain a formal style.

- Provide a concluding statement or section that follows from the argument presented.

To see examples of how teachers implement these and other grade-specific standards in their classrooms, turn to Section II of this book.

Needless to say, the introduction of the CCSS raises many questions for teachers and other instructional leaders. New mandates such as the CCSS can generate misconceptions and even myths, so it is important to look at the standards themselves. Because the implementation of the CCSS is an ongoing process, and because assessment is still under development, the online community associated with this book provides updates as well as a place to share ideas and experiences.

**Web 1.3**

### What is the relationship between the CCSS and the standards my state has already developed?

There may well be some overlap between the CCSS and the standards developed by your state, particularly when you look at the more global goals of the Anchor Standards. Because it is possible to supplement the CCSS with up to 15 percent of state standards, some state standards may be preserved, but generally in states that have formally adopted the CCSS these new standards will replace existing state ones. The timing of implementing CCSS varies from one state to another, with some states shifting immediately and others doing it over a year or two.

There are some distinct differences between the CCSS and state standards:

- First, they are intended to be used by all states so that students across the United States will be expected to achieve similar goals, even though they may reach them by different routes.

- The interdisciplinary emphasis of including literacy standards for history, science, social studies, and technical subjects in grades 6–12 makes the CCSS different from most state ELA standards.

- The CCSS emphasize *rigor* and connect it with what is called *textual complexity*, a term that refers to levels of meaning, quantitative readability measures, and reader variables such as motivation and experience.

- The CCSS position students as increasingly independent learners, frequently describing tasks they should perform "without assistance."

**Will the CCSS create a national curriculum?**

No. CCSS focuses on results, on what students should know and be able to do rather than the specific means for achieving learning goals. As the introduction to the CCSS states on page 4, "the Standards leave room for teachers, curriculum developers, and states to determine how those goals should be reached and what additional topics should be addressed. . . . Teachers are thus free to provide students with whatever tools and knowledge their professional judgment and experience identify as most helpful for meeting the goals set out in the Standards." In other words, the CCSS focus on what students should take away from schooling, but they stipulate that teachers should decide what to teach, how to teach it, and when and for how long to teach it. The CCSS acknowledge that teachers know what students bring to the classroom and how they learn best. Ongoing professional development, especially communities of learning with colleagues, will ensure that teachers have the content knowledge and expertise with instructional strategies to foster effective student learning.

**I've heard that the CCSS includes lists of *exemplar* texts. Isn't that going to create a national curriculum?**

The CCSS do include lists of texts on page 58 that illustrate what is called *text complexity* for each grade-level band. At the 6–8 level, for instance, the texts include both literary and informational texts. Among the literary selections are *Little Women* by Louisa May Alcott, "The Road Not Taken" by Robert Frost, *The Adventures of Tom Sawyer* by Mark Twain, *The Dark Is Rising* by Susan Cooper, *Dragonwings* by Lawrence Yep, and *Roll of Thunder, Hear My Cry* by Mildred Taylor. Informational texts include "Letter on Thomas Jefferson" by John Adams, *Narrative of the Life of Frederick Douglass, an American Slave* by Frederick Douglass, "Blood, Toil, Tears, and Sweat: Address to Parliament on May 13th, 1940" by Winston Churchill, *Harriet Tubman: Conductor on the Underground Railroad* by Ann Petry, and *Travels with Charley: In Search of America* by John Steinbeck.

**Web 1.4**

However, these texts are simply offered as examples of topics and genres that teachers might include, not as specific texts to be adopted in all classrooms. Teachers need to select texts appropriate for their own students and for the context in which they work. As the vignettes in Section II show, teachers can use a variety of texts to address the CCSS—Christopher Paul Curtis's *The Watsons Go to Birmingham—1963* and S. E. Hinton's *The Outsiders* are just two of them. The vignettes also show that these central or fulcrum texts work best when surrounded by contextual and texture texts that add perspective and meaning. For example, *The Outsiders* takes on new dimensions when read next to excerpts from Walter Dean Myers's *Monster* and news clippings about gang violence in contemporary society.

### What more do we know about text complexity?

In Appendix A, page 4, the CCSS define text complexity as "level of meaning, structure, language conventionality and clarity, knowledge demands, word frequency, sentence length [all in the context of] student knowledge, motivation and interest." This definition is expanded in a three-part model—qualitative dimensions, quantitative dimensions, and reader and task considerations. The quantitative dimension refers to features, such as word length or frequency, sentence length, and cohesion, that can be calculated by computers. The qualitative dimension refers to levels of meaning, structure, language conventions, and knowledge demands that cannot be measured well by machines but require careful attention from experienced readers/teachers. The reader and task considerations in Appendix A, page 4 include student motivation, knowledge, and experience as well as the purpose for reading, again, features that can be discerned by teachers "employing their professional judgment, experience and knowledge of their students and the subject."

It is worth noting that the CCSS acknowledge the limitations of this model of text complexity, particularly for literary forms such as poetry. Quantitative measures, for example, simply don't provide useful information about the relative complexity of a poem. Nor do they provide a useful measure of the complexity of much narrative fiction. As the CCSS observe in Appendix A, page 8, "some widely used quantitative measures, including the Flesch-Kincaid Grade Level test and the Lexile Framework for Reading, rate the Pulitzer Prize–winning novel *Grapes of Wrath* as appropriate for grades 2–3." This means that teachers need to play a key role in deciding what constitutes textual complexity for their students.

### What does *rigor* mean in this context?

Rigor is used in relation to text complexity. For example, in describing the reading standards for literature on pages 11 and 36, the CCSS include this sentence: "Rigor is also infused through the requirement that students read increasingly complex texts through the grades." Rigor refers to the goal of helping students to continue developing their capacities as readers so that with each passing year they build upon skills and understandings developed during the previous year.

Teachers who immerse their students in rich textual environments, require increasing amounts of reading, and help students choose ever more challenging texts will address rigor as it is defined by the CCSS. This means keeping students at the center, motivating them to continually develop as writers and readers, and engaging them in literacy projects that are relevant to their lives. When students feel personal connections, they are much more willing to wrestle with complex topics/texts/questions. Student engagement, then, offers the best route to rigor.

### Will implementing the CCSS mean eliminating literature in favor of "informational texts"?

It is true that the CCSS give significant attention to nonfiction, and on page 5, the introduction includes this statement: "Fulfilling the standards . . . requires much greater attention to a specific category of informational text—literary nonfiction." According to the CCSS, the amount of nonfiction should be increased as students mature so that by the time they are seniors in high school 70 percent of their reading should be nonfiction. But it is also true that the CCSS describe literacy development as a responsibility to be shared by teachers across multiple disciplines, so this doesn't mean that 70 percent of reading in ELA classes should be nonfiction. The standards for history/social studies, science, and technological subjects demonstrate how responsibility for reading nonfiction should be spread across multiple courses.

To reinforce this point, on page 5, the CCSS introduction underscores the importance of teaching literature: "Because the ELA classroom must focus on literature (stories, drama, and poetry) as well as literary nonfiction, a great deal of informational reading . . . must take place in other classes." The CCSS advocate the combination of adding more nonfiction to the curriculum in history/social studies, science, and technical subjects along with including more nonfiction in ELA classes. This combination still leaves plenty of space for literature in ELA classes.

### Do the CCSS advocate separating reading, writing, speaking, listening, and language from one another?

No. Although the standards are listed separately, the CCSS propose an integrated model of literacy. On page 4, the introduction explains, "Although the Standards are divided into Reading, Writing, Speaking and Listening, and Language strands for conceptual clarity, the processes of communication are closely connected as reflected throughout this document. For example, Writing Standard 9 requires that students be able to write about what they read." This integrated approach fits well with NCTE principles and with the ELA standards developed by many states.

### Formative evaluation is becoming increasingly important in my school. How do the CCSS address this?

Since the assessment portion of the CCSS is currently under development, it is impossible to know how it will address formative evaluation. The preliminary descriptions offered by the PARCC assessment consortium use the phrase "through course components" which is described as "actionable data that teachers can use to plan and adjust instruction." This suggests that formative evaluation could well be part of the CCSS assessment.

This could be good news because formative evaluation is assessment *for* learning, not assessment *of* learning. When assessment helps teachers understand where students are having difficulty, as well as where they understand clearly, it is possible to adjust instruction to address the areas of difficulty. Research shows that formative assessment can be a powerful means of improving achievement, particularly for students who typically don't do well in school.

Because assessments for the CCSS will be under development until 2014, it is worthwhile to monitor and perhaps contribute to their evolving shape.

**Web 1.5**

The websites for PARCC and SMARTER Balanced each include a list of the "governing states," and once you have determined which consortium your state is participating in, you can get in touch with the state representative(s) to learn more.

## What do the CCSS say about English language learners and/or students with special needs?

In a section titled "What Is Not Covered by the Standards" on page 6, the CCSS explain, "It is also beyond the scope of the Standards to define the full range of supports appropriate for English language learners and for students with special needs. At the same time, all students must have the opportunity to learn and meet the same high standards if they are to access the knowledge and skills necessary in their post-high school lives." This section goes on to say, "Each grade will include students who are still acquiring English. For those students, it is possible to meet the standards in reading, writing, speaking and listening without displaying native-like control of conventions and vocabulary." Based on this, we might assume some flexibility in applying the CCSS to English language learners.

The statement on page 6 about students with special needs takes a similar position: "The Standards should also be read as allowing for the widest possible range of students to participate fully from the outset and as permitting appropriate accommodations to ensure maximum participation of students with special education needs." Clearly the CCSS provide only limited guidance for implementing the standards with English language learners and students with special needs.

## Am I wrong to think that the CCSS will undercut teacher authority?

Probably. The CCSS make frequent reference to teachers' professional judgment and emphasize that teachers and other instructional leaders should be making many of the crucial decisions about student learning. The implementation of CCSS by individual states and/or school districts could have negative consequences for teachers, and it is impossible to know what will result from the as-yet-undeveloped assessment of the CCSS.

Still, in the best case, the CCSS can offer benefits to teachers. They can make it easier for teachers to deal with transient students by assuring that they have been working toward similar goals in their previous school. The CCSS can provide a lens through which teachers can examine their own practice to find areas that would benefit from more instructional attention or to introduce more balance into the curriculum. A number of teachers have reported that state standards had such effects, and it is reasonable to think that the CCSS might function similarly. Most of all, the CCSS can provide an occasion for teachers to consider what constitutes the most effective ELA teaching.

## What is NCTE's stake in the CCSS?

Although it commented on drafts of the CCSS when they were under development, NCTE did not participate in creating these standards. As an association most directly concerned with professional development, NCTE is invested in supporting teachers as they face the challenges posed by the CCSS. In addition, it is an association that values teacher voices, like the ones included in Section II of this volume. To that end, the Executive Committee of NCTE commissioned and invested in the four-volume set to which this book belongs. NCTE is also devoting online resources to providing materials that extend beyond this book and provide a space where communities of teachers can share ideas and strategies.

## How should I begin to deal with the CCSS?

As the introduction to this book suggests, it makes sense to begin with students because teachers know more about their students than anyone else. As a first step you might make a list of goals for the students you are teaching now. Consider the skills, dispositions, motivations, habits, and abilities you would like them to develop. Your list probably encompasses every standard in the CCSS along with a good deal more. Keep your entire list in mind as you approach the CCSS, and start by thinking about what your students need to learn.

Looking at the learning needs of students in light of the CCSS can lead, in turn, to considering classroom practices and thinking about how various instructional strategies might be refined or adapted to foster student learning. Looking at classroom practices leads to questions about instructional materials and, ultimately, the curriculum. Woven through all of these is the continuing theme of professional growth and development because asking questions and reconsidering nearly always require changes that are best supported by professional development.

The Common Core State Standards (CCSS) may feel like yet another set of top-down, mandated standards. And integrating the CCSS into the curricula and teaching can, at times, generate feelings of pressure and conflict. But it is also possible to approach the CCSS from a different perspective as well—one that sees opportunities for bridging between good practice based on NCTE principles and policy and what the CCSS offer. The NCTE community, of which this book series is a part, is one space where you can start to build bridges and frame your interactions with the CCSS in ways that are empowering, highlight and encourage best practices in literacy learning, and sustain the incredible work that English teachers are already doing in classrooms. Rather than focusing on how the CCSS will subvert the instruction we are already doing, framing our approach to the standards instead around observing, contextualizing, and building can help us to bridge the CCSS and established instructional practices based on NCTE principles, allowing the two to work in tandem.

First, one way to frame discussions about and approaches to the CCSS is to focus on detailed observation. Before we can become teachers who incorporate these standards in meaningful and pedagogically sound ways into our practices, we need to be learners who observe and take careful note of what exists in the document and what the standards are asking of students. We also need to develop observational lenses through which to see the standards that will keep students and their needs at the center of all instructional change. Learning about the CCSS through close observation may better equip us to advocate for our students' unique needs.

A second way to think about the standards is to use them as a frame for contextualizing. It is important to remember that, while we observe and take note of what exists in the CCSS document itself, we always need to keep specific school and classroom cultures and environments in mind, understanding how different teaching contexts can pose different challenges and opportunities. The teaching vignettes you will read in this section seek to display and honor a variety of school contexts, cultures, and teaching environments, but not all of the teachers in this volume approach planning with the CCSS in the same way, and their lessons don't look the same. A consideration of local context, then, must be coupled with detailed observation of the CCSS document itself.

Third, we can see the CCSS as a frame for building our instruction and classrooms and for meeting students where they are and keeping their needs at the center of lesson design and instruction. To build with the CCSS in mind, we need to begin to see them as more than boxes to check off on a list or forces mandated from above that are seeking to destroy our classrooms. Instead, building *from* and at times *with* the CCSS will involve developing knowledge about the document itself, examining and evaluating our current experiences in the classroom and the culture in which we teach, and relying on the communities around us for support and assistance.

This book, then, is framed around observing the CCSS closely, contextualizing these standards to address specific students in specific schools, and building instruction that integrates the CCSS with NCTE principles for teaching English language arts.

## Observing

Detailed observation of the CCSS can begin with identifying where the standards may present shifts from previous state standards documents and identifying patterns in the language of the CCSS document. By looking across the document in this way, you can see some of the most salient shifts. Below, you will find a brief overview of student-focused shifts and instructional shifts that occur in the CCSS document, as well as references to specific CCSS document pages where you can seek greater specificity about these themes.

### Student-Focused Shifts

- *Meaning-making*—The CCSS require that students will do more than just read texts for basic comprehension; instead, students will be expected to pull from multiple sources to synthesize diverse texts and ideas, consider multiple points of view, and read across texts. (See, for example, pages 8 and 40 of the CCSS document.)

- *Developing independence*—The ultimate goal of each standard is that all students will demonstrate the ability to enact key skills and strategies articulated in the CCSS on their own. To help students reach this goal, the CCSS spiral expectations across grade levels. Standards for the elementary grades, for example, include language about how students should enact the standard "with support." To clarify, this expectation does not diminish the need to scaffold instruction at all grade levels; rather, the goal is to move students toward independent enactment of standards. (See CCSS document, page 7. Note that while there are times when the language of independence is explicitly stated as on page 55, this expectation is also embedded in assumptions about all CCSS).

- *Transfer of learning*—On page 7, the CCSS state that students will be required to respond to a variety of literacy demands within their content area courses—ELA *and* others—and to discuss with others how their ability to meet these demands will prepare them for the demands they will face in college and in their future careers.

- *College and career readiness*—Linked to transfer, on page 7, the CCSS expectations articulate a rationale for what college- and career-ready high school students will be able to do. There is little, if any, focus on rote memorization. Rather, the CCSS focus is on skills, strategies, and habits that will enable students to adapt to the rhetorical demands of their future learning and contributions.

## Instructional Shifts

It is important to reiterate that the CCSS do not mandate *how* teachers should teach; this is even stated explicitly on page 6 in the document. Why a focus on instructional shifts? Clearly, just as the CCSS spell out what students will be expected to do, the CCSS may prompt shifts in our thinking about how best to help students meet these expectations, which will inevitably affect our teaching.

- *Spiraling instruction*—Unlike some state and district standards, the CCSS do not promote instructional coverage. Instead, the CCSS invite spiraled instruction. Students will be expected to enact particular standards repeatedly within grade-level content area courses *and* across grade levels. In part, this is evident when tracing the lineage of a particular standard to the grade level below and above. Parts of particular CCSS are repeated and built on in subsequent grades. The CCSS are therefore meant to build iteratively. On page 30 of the CCSS document there is a graphic representation of this spiraling idea with regard to language skills, but a similar graphic could just as well be created to illustrate the approach to the other ELA threads as well. For further discussion of spiraling instruction, see Section III of this volume.

- *Integration of ELA threads*—On pages 4 and 47, the CCSS encourage an "integrated model of literacy" whereby ELA threads (e.g., reading and writing) are woven throughout units of study.

- *Inclusion of nonfiction or informational texts*—On page 5, the CCSS set explicit expectations regarding the kinds of texts students read and write. By twelfth grade, 70 percent of the sum of students' reading, for example, is to be informational, nonfiction reading. But as we discuss further in Section III, the responsibility for this reading is shared by all content area teachers. Still, the inclusion of more informational text may present a shift for some.

- *Text complexity*—Page 57 of the CCSS document offers a descriptive graphic on text complexity. NCTE principles affirm the range of ways that strong ELA teachers introduce increasingly complex texts to student readers. These include but are not limited to student interest, genre, language, content, and ELA concepts foregrounded in instruction.

# II

# Contextualizing

# Inquiry and Independence in the English Language Arts Classroom

# 2

## Meet Tonya Perry, University of Alabama at Birmingham

In this section of the book, you will be introduced to six teachers who work with middle school students in their English and/or reading classes every day. We will learn more about their teaching and how they integrate the CCSS into their instruction. Through their experiences, perhaps you will learn more about framing the CCSS in your context and find some useful ways to build on curriculum that already affects student learning. We will read how these teachers continue to make learning come alive for their students and, at the same time, face the challenges that often accompany integrating a new set of standards.

In my teaching journey that started more than twenty years ago, I have focused mainly in the middle grades. I have been taught powerful lessons by these young adolescents. One of the most powerful recurring lessons has been the importance of relevance in my teaching. This takes on so many different aspects: selection of text, choice, engagement, community building, differentiation, and connectedness. No matter the new challenge in education, the idea of relevance remains at the core of my teaching. This does not mean that students recycle information that they already know; the challenge is to connect the new learning to something that already exists—to scaffold that learning. I think the CCSS give us the opportunity to have conversations about relevance and connections with horizontal and vertical teaching with colleagues; otherwise, teaching will be disjointed and lack the "spiraled" design that is so important in the thinking behind the CCSS.

We do not have to choose between the CCSS and the students' need for relevance and connectedness, but I do think educators will have to think carefully and collaborate about what we want students to know and how we are instructing them to increase their learning. Although the standards call for increased informational reading, dialogue about how to do this and conversations about the personal reading and writing needs of students can coexist. The answer is there for us to discover in the context of our classrooms along with teachers in the content areas.

Three of the teachers from this volume and I spent much time together discussing the CCSS. Each is from a different school, bringing an even broader perspective about the infusion of the standards into the classroom. We have learned from each other just how beneficial it is to expand the professional community beyond the school walls through our dialogue as educators and our ties as Red Mountain Writing Project Fellows. My co-contributors Anne Gere and Rebecca Manery brought other teachers into the conversation and our circle of thinking expanded. Through conversations and NCTE Web seminars, all of these teachers and I have increased our knowledge about the CCSS exponentially. As a result, we share with you our thinking throughout the text before each pair of vignettes you will read.

All the teachers in this volume have generously invited us into their classrooms to experience teaching and learning moments that illustrate how the chaos of their classroom life is indeed deliberate, precise, and carefully designed. The teaching and learning practices described highlight the ways these teachers work to enact NCTE principles that affirm the value of the knowledge and experience students bring to school, the role of equity in literacy learning, and—always—the learning needs of students while attending to the CCSS. Each of the teaching and learning vignettes within each chapter is preceded by a brief description of the context in which the teacher and his or her students are working and is followed by an explanation of the teacher's journey to developing pathways to enact these practices because, as we all know, exemplary moments in teaching are the product of many years of studying classroom practice, discussing ideas with colleagues, and reflecting on teaching and learning. Charts following the vignettes highlight key teaching and learning practices and connect them with specific CCSS and with NCTE research-based principles; footnotes point toward research that supports the teaching described; and finally, in the "Frames That Build" sections, I offer exercises to help you think about how the teaching and learning practices highlighted in the vignettes can connect to your local teaching context.

The online component of this book offers additional classroom vignettes along with questions to prompt reflection and generate conversations among readers who want to deepen their understanding of their students and expand their professional knowledge of literacy theory and practice.

# Contextualizing

The way we design instruction with local context and the CCSS in mind determines the kind of learning that will emerge on the canvas of our classrooms. What we emphasize, what we say, and what we spend our time engaged in will emerge in what and how our students learn. So, we are deliberate, knowing that what happens on the first day and how it connects to the last day matters. We are precise, cognizant that the language of learning permeating our classrooms affects thinking.

It is our hope that these teaching and learning vignettes and the corresponding materials will serve as a reflection of the language of learning that already fills your classrooms, and that they will demonstrate a framework that allows thinking about not just *what* we do, but *why* we do it. We hope they will remind us that in the layers of local, state, and national values, the greatest intentionality comes from the classroom teacher who enters the complexity and emerges with a process that honors the learning in our classrooms. We invite you to step into these classrooms, reflect on them, and use their successes and challenges to further your own thinking about what bridges you can build between the CCSS and your own instruction.

During one group session about the CCSS, teachers and I discussed the benefits of facilitating middle schoolers' development as more independent thinkers. The College and Career Readiness guidelines in the CCSS call for students who demonstrate independence, and part of that process is decision-making about their own time, choosing references and support, and discerning key points and ideas (p. 7). In this next section, you will see two teachers, Kathleen and Rod, who guide their students through the inquiry process. Kathleen implements the reading and writing workshop, allowing students to plan their independent work for the day based on personal inquiry. Rod allows students to choose a social issue of importance to them and conduct independent inquiries about the issues they choose. This type of instruction helps students engage in their own learning process to develop important skills, such as researching, revising, and questioning their own choices and the larger world around them.

As you read through the chapters in this volume, look for the following symbols to signal various themes and practices.

**Common Core State Standards**

**Collaboration**

**Connections**

**Integrated Teaching and Learning**

**Honoring Diversity**

**Connections**

Section III focuses exclusively on the building frame. There, you will find specific resources for building your instruction with the CCSS and for working with colleagues to observe patterns in the CCSS document compared to previous local and state standards.

## Meet Kathleen Hayes-Parvin, Birney Middle School

Kathleen Hayes-Parvin is currently facing many challenges that result from the declining economy of the community where her school is located. The unemployment rate is over 18 percent, the school district had to cut $20 million from its budget

last year, and the school is facing additional cuts this year. Children in the community are struggling: home foreclosures, unemployment, and fractured families have increased the transience of the student population. At this Title I school, approximately 45 percent of the students receive free or reduced-price lunch. Many of them cannot afford basic school supplies, and Kathleen often goes to the Dollar Store to buy pencils and erasers for them. A number of school services have been outsourced, which limits the opportunities available to students. Late buses, for example, have been eliminated as a cost-cutting measure by the private company that now handles transportation, so many students cannot participate in after-school activities or stay to get extra help from teachers.

The effects of family poverty and diminished school resources take their toll on students, as Kathleen learns from their writing and from conversations. She often reads accounts of families moving in with relatives or having to go to food banks. Not surprisingly, Kathleen finds that a number of her students are less school-congruent than those she taught several years ago, and this difference is exacerbated by the financial constraints faced by her school district. She used to teach on a block schedule and have classes of about twenty-six students, but this year the block schedule was eliminated, and class sizes were increased to thirty, so she is teaching 150 sixth graders every day. The school, formerly a middle school, has been transformed into a K–8 building because of dropping enrollments in the district, and a new pull-out program takes a number of the most talented students out of the regular classes that Kathleen teaches. Yet, Kathleen finds ways to meet the challenges of working in an under-resourced school. She is good at finding ways to compensate for the dwindling financial support, often calling on a network of friends and former teachers to help underwrite the cost of books and other classroom materials. She views families as allies in their children's education, giving them a variety of ways to become involved in her classroom. She takes advantage of community resources, incorporating the public library's Battle of Books into her curriculum and offering local businesses opportunities to support school projects. Kathleen's goal is for each of her students to be active learners who will become "real readers and real writers." By "real" Kathleen means emulating the practices of literacy professionals. These goals emerged from Kathleen's experience with the National Writing Project, where she began to see herself as a writer, and she wants her students to have the same opportunity. Her earlier background in special

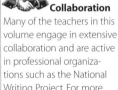 **Collaboration**

Many of the teachers in this volume engage in extensive collaboration and are active in professional organizations such as the National Writing Project. For more ideas about how to work collaboratively with colleagues and your local community, see the resources in Section III of this text.

education strengthened her commitment to helping students develop their capacities for meaning-making in reading, and her collaboration with teaching partners in her school and teacher colleagues across the state has further strengthened her desire to help students become real readers and real writers.

## Integrating Reading and Writing: Kathleen's Classroom

Kathleen's third-period class comes into a room filled with books. There are bookshelves pushed against every wall, low ones and high ones; recently she asked her students to help count all the books in the classroom, and they found 577. In addition to the desks where students sit, there is a comfortable sofa surrounded by cushions. On every metal surface there are magnetic letters and words arranged into poems. Several class mottos are displayed on the walls: "Read and write every day"; "Ten points a day = an A"; "If you're not making meaning, you're not reading"; and "If you don't come with what you need, I can't help you succeed." In one corner sits an expensive projector and a visual presenter. The visual presenter was donated by a local corporation, but it didn't come with a projector. Kathleen was able to buy the projector because one of her students won an essay contest in a local competition called Dough for Teachers, and the prize included a grant for Kathleen to use for classroom supplies.

As her third-period class enters the classroom, Kathleen greets each student by name and invites him or her to take a seat. As soon as everyone is settled, she begins talking about their writer's notebooks, praising them for writing every day. Then she mentions that she has been seeing some common problems in their writing. One of these is difficulty with the *their/there/they're* distinction, so she does a mini-lesson to explain how each one is used, urging students to watch for these in their reading at the same time that they work on using the correct word in their writing. She also encourages students to focus on readability as they are writing.

> **Integrated Teaching and Learning**
>
> Kathleen teaches the conventions of Standard Written English in the context of student writing, integrating writing and language instruction so that students can make connections between language use and writing situations.

After the mini-lesson is over, Kathleen asks students to respond to "status of the class," where all students list what they have accomplished in their homework and what they will work on during class. A few students who have received praise for meeting homework writing goals ask if they can sit on the sofa or one of the cushions, and Kathleen agrees. Most students move comfortably into independent work. Some are doing revisions, others are composing in their writer's notebook, and still others are writing first drafts. Kathleen links student writing to reading, and since they just read a memoir, they are writing memoirs. A few students have difficulty getting started, and Kathleen asks them questions about what they plan to accomplish. One student needs to select a new book, and Kathleen leads him over to a bookshelf, reminding him, "Your last book was *Diary of a Wimpy Kid.*

**Honoring Diversity**

Kathleen's approach to independent reading time allows her to differentiate instruction for students at different levels and stages of their writing process. It also allows her to check in on students' progress—an informal formative assessment that will help her plan for instruction later.

**Honoring Diversity**

Kathleen involves families in their students' learning by sharing successes. This acknowledges students as diverse individuals and enables Kathleen to maintain positive contact with students' families and home lives.

Remember we call that a 'potato chip' book. You should choose something more substantial this time, something that will give you new ideas for writing." After the student chooses his book, she begins conferences with students, asking individuals to sit next to her to show her or read aloud what they have written, and Kathleen asks questions and makes suggestions in response.

Near the end of the class there is a call from the office, explaining that a student named Jamal Brown should come down for early dismissal. Kathleen responds by asking, "Is Jamal's dad here?" and when the answer is affirmative, she says, "Does he have time to come to the classroom?" Jamal, one of the students who had difficulty getting started on his writing, has been working steadily, and Kathleen had just read and praised the latest entry in his writer's notebook. Furthermore, Jamal had come to class with all his materials, and his weekly packet was complete, on time, and entries were numbered, dated, and in chronological order, all important to the accountability that is central in a workshop class. When Mr. Brown enters the room, Kathleen says, "I wanted you to come here and see the great work Jamal is doing." She reads a short selection from the notebook and explains what makes it good. Jamal, whom Kathleen later describes as an ADHD student whose work had taken a serious downturn in her class, jumps up and down, saying "I'm back. I'm back."

## Kathleen's Journey: Pathways to Enact These Practices

Kathleen's professional development as a teacher has included multiple opportunities to work with colleagues in her district as well as across the state. She participated in the Summer Institute of a National Writing Project site in 1992, and this experience led her to begin using a workshop approach to teach writing. "This was where I really began to understand authentic writing," she claims. "NWP made me a writer, and I wanted my students to have the same experience." Subsequently, she also took part in designing state English language arts standards, working with colleagues from many school districts to determine what students should know and be able to do. Kathleen refers to this experience as one that furthered her professional development. "I learned so much from those conversations; discussing goals with other teachers gave me a whole new perspective in my own classroom," she says. As the population and circumstances of her school have changed, Kathleen has continued to develop new strategies and approaches. She attends state and national meetings of NCTE, she confers with colleagues within and beyond her school, and she reads continually to add to her classroom library. Most recently, she has spent two of the past five summers studying workshop approaches with Lucy Calkins.

She attributes her long and substantial commitment to the workshop approach to the ways it fosters student achievement in writing. She says, "It creates a space where young writers can pursue their guided choices and begin to gain the knowledge that they are becoming real writers by approximating the actions of other writers." She also praises workshop for the way it embraces differentiated instruction, enabling her to meet the needs of students with a wide variety of abilities as readers and writers.

Another area of development has been what she calls teaching parents/guardians. "I'm not just teaching 150 kids," she says, "I need to educate parents, too." Because she knows that home support for student learning is critical, she makes it a point to establish contact with home at the beginning of the school year. Earlier in her career she called homes, but now she sends emails to homes, describing what students will be doing in her class and what she expects them to accomplish. Throughout the year she uses every available opportunity to maintain a school–home connection, and her response to Mr. Brown in the vignette above is typical. If a parent comes to the school to drop off a lunch or gym shoes or pick up a child for early dismissal, she always invites the parent into the classroom. By showing parents what students can accomplish in writing, she wins their support and rarely has to answer questions about why she doesn't use grammar worksheets.

Kathleen is confident that her approach to teaching will enable students to meet the CCSS. After all, as she notes, she has moved successfully from state standards and benchmarks to grade-level expectations, and in every case her students have continued to perform well on required tests.

It is common for students in Kathleen's classes to advance several grade levels in reading and to become fluent writers. "My students are absolutely marinated in literacy," she claims. "Because they do so much reading and writing every day, they don't have a lot of difficulty meeting standards." She is more concerned about providing high-quality education in an under-resourced environment, and she focuses on becoming more resourceful in getting books, materials, and enriching experiences for her students.

In an effort to help her students take a larger and more positive view of education, she maintains a partnership with a local university, and her students regularly meet with undergraduates. This partnership extends back at least fifteen years, and it grew out of Kathleen's experience as a cooperating teacher for undergraduates in a teacher education program. After opening her classroom to prospective teachers who observed her innovative instruction, Kathleen arranged to take her students to visit campus. In addition to seeing buildings, visiting the natural history museum, and eating in a dorm, her sixth graders met with the prospective teachers to offer advice and answer questions about how they could become more effective with middle school students. This experience enhanced Kathleen's students' perception of themselves as readers and writers, but it also expanded their view of themselves as learners.

She encouraged them to think about going to college by making it more real for them. When her students first emerged from the bus after arriving on campus, one boy turned to Kathleen and asked, "Which building is the university in?" When she responded, "all of them," this youngster took one more step toward seeing himself as a college student. In concert with university colleagues, Kathleen has modified the shape of these interactions several times over the years, but this experience, like the workshop approach, is foundational to her teaching. As she says, "When my sixth graders learn about and implement 'best practices in ELA' and prepare to share their work on an evening in Ann Arbor with soon-to-be-teachers, they feel that they too are teachers and will have an impact on a young teacher's practice and on perhaps all of the young learners to come." Part of the impact of this experience comes from the writing Kathleen's students do about it, initially in their notebooks and later sharing with the entire class. Kathleen is committed to continuing growth and development as a teacher, but she is even more deeply committed to the learning of her students.

## Meet Rod Leonard, Smith Middle School

Rod is a fifth-year teacher in an urban middle school in a large southeastern city. The school district enrolls about 25,000 students per year and has a faculty of approximately 1,900 teachers. At his school, Rod teaches seventh-grade English language arts. The school enrolls 400 students with a 96 percent African American population, and 81 percent of the students are eligible for free and reduced-price lunch. On average, twenty-four to thirty students attend class in fifty-minute blocks.

Rod's school is proud of its accomplishments and history. The school has earned national recognition as a High Flying School. In addition, the school earned two project renovation awards: Hibbett Sports Project and NBA Cares in partnership with BBVA Compass Bank. The principal, Dr. Willis, is a Milken Award–winning instructional leader who prides himself on developing teachers who can use research and performance data to determine best practices for the students. Dr. Willis promotes Project Based Learning (PBL) and differentiated instruction among his faculty, providing support through workshops and professional development opportunities on a consistent basis. Accustomed to a history of academic success, parents and community members expect the students to perform well despite the challenges that schools sometimes face (budget cuts, limited resources, larger class sizes, etc.).

Rod has been recognized by his principals as an effective teacher who positively affects student learning. His creative teaching style and interaction with students help them understand the content. However, despite his teaching success, Rod sometimes has reservations about what students can do amid such seemingly insurmountable challenges. He has only one class set of a three-year-old textbook for 125 students, so he cannot assign homework with them. The budget for the district, and the state, for that matter, has been cut significantly, so basic resources, such as paper, scissors, tape, and glue, are not as plentiful as in years past. District-mandated testing has increased in recent years, and even though teachers recognize that it is valuable to measure student growth, it sometimes feels like testing is taking more and more time away from instruction. This has affected teacher morale, parent involvement, and student pride, leaving a once energetic group a little disheartened by the circumstances.

These circumstances gradually affected Rod's teaching and at the beginning of the year, feeling test-weary, he started teaching his students standard by standard to make sure that the course of study was covered. He wanted to make sure that the objectives on the diagnostic tests, especially the ones that were missed by a majority of the students, were explicitly taught for extended periods of time. Each day the standard was the focus, not the holistic instruction. Rod noticed early in the year just how disinterested his students were becoming in their response to class. Students were strolling in the classroom close to the tardy bell. He also noticed his own lack of energy in his delivery of the content. Reading a passage from a text to find the main idea, Rod recalls losing his place and none of the students could help him recall where he was in the section. He felt as if he and the students were sinking. Rod quickly realized that this type of teaching, standard by standard, was not best for him or his students. He began to redesign his instruction for students to learn in more authentic ways after a summer with the Red Mountain Writing Project.

> **Integrated Teaching and Learning**
>
> After attempting to "teach to the standards," Rod learned that his teaching and the students' learning suffered from this approach. Engaging in frequent reflection and critical analysis of teaching practice can help teachers shift their approach when and where necessary.

## Connecting Literacy to Life: Rod's Classroom

Reinvigorated, Rod wanted his students to make connections with the outside world using writing as an authentic vehicle. Along with a university colleague, he designed a Social Justice Photo Journal unit to give voice to students about their world. The adapted idea was loosely based on an article from *English Journal*: "Seeing English in the City: Using Photography to Understand Students' Literacy Relationships." Rod and his colleague began to think about this concept in the middle school context. How could young adolescents do more with their literacy skills to affect their city? Designing the end of the unit first, the two began to plan. They decided that students should be able to create a portfolio of pictures and words that illustrated their chosen social issue. Students should be able to reflect on the issue, describe the issue (pictures and words), and persuade stakeholders to help address the issue. This portfolio, they decided, would be a culmination of literacy skills, a two-week unit with integrated standards and objectives. The end result of the unit was designed for students to use writing and reading to positively affect their communities.

On the first day of the unit, Rod started class by asking students to write a journal entry about problems they see in their community. Before students wrote, he verbally modeled an example for them to better understand the expectations. After the students wrote, he allowed them to pair-share their responses. Rod rotated to different pairs in the room, listening to students discuss their entries. He then showed a YouTube clip from United Way, asking students to listen for additional societal challenges from the video participants. Rod recognized the importance of teaching students to view and critique media. Processing the new information gathered from the video clip, students then returned to their desks to add any problems that they had not addressed in their initial writing assignment. Students shared again in pairs.

Students ranked the issues according to their importance. Students numbered 1 to 5 on their papers, which helped them narrow their focus. Rod then asked students to circle the top choice and asked them to think about the issue in depth. Students then created questions about the one topic that interested them most.

Then Rod moved students into their Café Conversations. A model based on a coffeehouse setting, Café Conversations allowed students to discuss issues in a relaxed environment to encourage authentic talk and exchange of thoughts. Rod used this technique for students to gain insight from peers about issues and to help narrow their individual focus for the unit. While drinking orange juice and eating doughnuts, students talked about their issues in pairs or triads, seeking input to their questions. Students chose topics such as homelessness, poverty, litter, school improvement, obesity, children with disabilities, violence, and business growth in the city. Students wanted to know the following:

- Why are so many businesses leaving the city? Who can help bring them back?

- Why do we have so many people who are homeless on benches? What about the shelters?

- What does being obese lead to?

- When people with disabilities get older, what can they do?

**Common Core State Standards**

Students produce clear and coherent journal entries to share with classmates, which addresses Writing Standard 4 of the CCSS. Students do this to clearly articulate their ideas about an issue, which they will later expand on through additional writing tasks.

**Honoring Diversity**

By allowing students to choose their own issues, Rod honors the diverse perspectives and life experiences his students bring to this learning task.

**Common Core State Standards**

Rod acknowledges through his Café Conversations that talk is important in the writing classroom. Opportunities to share, reflect, critique, and revisit a piece of writing affect students' products.

Rod then modeled the photojournalistic piece of the project. He shared that the first step to problem-solving is to realize that a problem exists. Without taking pictures of people or body parts, not even fingers, he wanted students to think of twenty different ways to illustrate their social issue through pictures. He showed his images of homelessness through pictures of sleeping areas under bridges, park benches, a "Need work" sign, shopping carts, a US flag, etc. Students discussed their understanding of each one, analyzing the images of homelessness and offering suggestions for improving them. Rod anticipated that this critical exchange would affect students' thinking about their own work. Visual literacies, like those in which Rod engages his students, are a powerful way for middle school students to express their understanding, critique their stance, and construct meaningful dialogue.

**Common Core State Standards**
Rod's students prepare inquiry questions to guide their research of their chosen topics. This meets writing standards and also scaffolds students' learning. This may also give Rod a chance to formatively assess his students' thought and writing processes.

Students then returned to their Café Conversations to create a list of pictures they could take to represent their social issues. Students shared ideas across topics and collected a functional list of items and places that could help them tell their story through photos. To end class, Rod used an author share approach. Students who needed additional ideas would sit on the stool in front of the class. They would explain their project to the class, read ideas for photos to depict an issue, and gain additional ideas from classmates to add to their list. The class brainstormed ideas as Rod facilitated the discussion. At the end of class, students began to think about stakeholders who could help them improve the condition of the city, school, or community. One student expressed the empowerment felt by the class, saying, "I am going to take pictures of the things we need fixed at our school and send my letter to the superintendent!"

On subsequent days, Rod required students to complete assignments that would help them learn more about their social issue and their impact in the community. Students participated in Concentric Circles (also referred to as Fishbowl) to discuss strategies for community impact. The smaller circle of students or the "inside circle" was asked to talk about their topics in detail with a partner. The larger circle of students or the "outside circle" was asked to listen carefully. When signaled, the two began to exchange ideas that students could use to affect the community. For example, when Lisa and Donald discussed adults with disabilities, they brainstormed together a fundraiser for additional ramps and supplies for people with disabilities. Another pair talked about homelessness and a school coat drive. Rod then signaled that it was time for the people in the "outside circle" to talk about their projects while the "inside circle" listened. More ideas surfaced from this exchange. Talk and collaboration were an integral part of the inquiry process. Students discussed their issues with classmates and sometimes

**Integrated Teaching and Learning**
Research has shown that talk is an important part of the writing and thinking process. In this Fishbowl activity, students are required to learn from one another as they think about their ideas and hear others' perspectives. They are also required to listen and provide feedback for their peers, which may affect their thoughts about their own projects.

challenged their classmates to think more deeply about issues. One student named a magazine picture of a secret camera "The Walls Have Eyes" as a way to prevent crime and make potential violators aware of the surveillance. Through discussion with his writing buddy, he was able to make a salient point that may have been undeveloped without the collaborative partnership.

Rod asked the students to think about who would be in the best position to help them develop their intervention projects. Each student researched agencies, government officials, school administrators, and community leaders who could assist them. With an audience in mind, students began to craft persuasive letters to the stakeholders about their important issues. The writing lesson started with the importance of knowing your audience to influence the greatest change. Rod and students talked about the importance of word choice and tone when writing a persuasive piece. He modeled an argumentative letter and, paragraph by paragraph, discussed the role of each section. Students commented on and critiqued Rod's writing based on clarity, effectiveness, tone, and basic writing skills. The students then began to draft their own versions of argumentative writing, using each other as peer readers.

## *Learning Skills through Inquiry: Rod's Journey*

Rod admits, "For a time there, I had underestimated what my students could do. I became so engrossed with teaching the standards and giving tests that I did not let my students' learning needs come first. The students have really surprised me with their thinking. Through this teaching experience [Social Justice Photo Journal unit], I have actually transitioned into more of a facilitator." As a facilitator, Rod monitored student learning and expected students to develop their own inquiries. He worked beside the students to encourage, direct, and enrich their understanding, but not to control their learning at every step. Rod realized the importance of student involvement in the learning process. During the Social Issues unit, students would actually ask about instruction for the day. ("What are we going to do today? Do we get our pictures back? Can I go to the computer lab? Can I finish my letter?") This was quite a different response from the usual "wait-on-the-teacher-to-teach-me" approach the students displayed prior to the unit. Rod had a greater appreciation for his students and what they could do. Sometimes, as teachers, we can get stuck in the day-to-day responsibilities of teaching: identifying the skills students do not know and reteaching them in isolation—checking off the objective boxes. Although this is needed at times, this should not take the place of the real-world, inquiry-based instruction that ties students to their context, enhances student thinking, and promotes endless questioning.

 **Collaboration**
Rod collaborates both with other teachers through the Red Mountain Writing Project and with administrators at his school and in his district, which gives him the support he needs to think critically about his teaching and try new things in the classroom.

Rod attends local professional development opportunities provided by the school district and local, state, and national conferences. As an advanced fellow for the Red Mountain Writing Project, he understands the importance of reading and writing in the classroom. Rod has participated in the Red Mountain Writing Project for two years. During each experience, he has learned more about integrating authentic literacy learning experiences into a classroom often guided by schoolwide formative assessments. Rod admits that it has been difficult to balance the type of inquiry instruction he knows will engage the students and promote learning in the midst of a demanding testing climate that measures skills. It is a constant see-saw motion for him, but through his work with the Writing Project and other professional development activities, such as Pre-Advanced Placement training and Problem-Based Learning, he is learning more about teaching students at high levels. He attributes much of his learning to his district administrator and principal who promote professional learning at all levels. "I pick up tidbits wherever I go. I absorb from other teachers."

Rod is a consummate learner himself who is always interested in improving his teaching. He has a mentor at school who is very supportive of his work. At the same time, he attends graduate school and works on projects with the Writing Project. Rod's learning community extends from his school teaching team to a national circle of teachers he interacts with through the National Council of Teachers of English and the National Writing Project. From his work in graduate school, Rod has learned more about differentiated instruction, ways to look at the learners as individuals rather than as a whole class. Rod has started using more grouping in his class to meet the needs of students. He also has incorporated varied texts in his class, ranging from magazines to visual resource texts, to support all learners. Rod believes the CCSS will help teachers have conversations across grade levels and subject areas about effective instruction for students. He acknowledges their complexity, also. "[Adapting to the CCSS] will not happen overnight. This new conversation about CCSS is going to take time, but we must have patience and be open-minded."

## Charting the Practices

As Kathleen and Rod illustrate, how we think and talk about learning speaks volumes about what we value. The teachers in these vignettes jointly value fostering students' lifelong learning and their development as readers and writers. As we illuminate a range of pathways by which teachers plan with this goal in mind, we would be negligent if we represented planning as a recipe with the same steps for all. In fact, our individual planning processes vary widely across time, courses, and students. Figure 2.1 represents the range of pathways, or processes, by which teachers consider the integration of their teaching and the learning they plan for students.

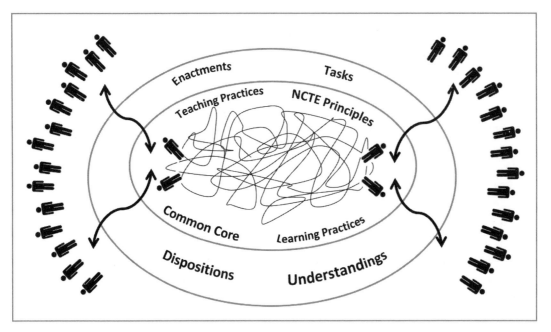

**FIGURE 2.1:** Pathways to planning and enacting instruction.

Through reflection or conversation, the teachers in these vignettes speak to some form of wrestling with chaos in describing their thinking about planning. Figure 2.1 represents the chaos that we all navigate, but it also seeks to honor the fact that how we enter this chaos—the pathways by which we get there—varies. Some teachers enter through knowledge about their students, which are represented in the figure as encompassing and informing our thinking. Some teachers enter by thinking about the ultimate goals they have for their students; these are represented in the language of the outer circle including the dispositions, understandings, tasks, and enactments teachers expect students to demonstrate or develop. No matter the entrance, once in the middle we ultimately navigate the chaos that involves carefullly considering the meeting place and relationship between these goals and the CCSS/NCTE principles, our teaching practices, and the learning practices we personally develop as well as those we foster in our students. The narratives offered by Kathleen and Rod affirm that we meet these considerations through different pathways over time.

Figure 2.1 visually represents the way we conceptualize these inextricably linked considerations that are at the heart of our decision making as teachers. We intentionally chose not to represent them as linear, and one of our earliest versions of this figure actually included the words in the inner circle embedded within the chaos of the nest at the middle. Given the difficulty of actually reading this chaos, we chose in favor of readability; however, the original visual may more accurately represent why at times it is difficult for us to articulate the complexity of our thinking, acting, and ongoing learning about how to work with and meet the needs of diverse learners. Still, we believe it is possible and quite critical that we work to identify our decision making as well as how we conceive of the elements that inform our decisions, especially as we remind ourselves and others that even as we prepare students to meet their standards, the CCSS do not dictate the path we choose.

We hope that you will keep Figure 2.1 in mind as you read the charts that follow and that you will find at the end of each vignette chapter. In these charts, we endeavor to represent how the instructional decisions that emerge out of the chaos are dynamic. For ease of representation, these charts read more linearly than the processes they depict. But they include the elements of our decision making and acting out of the chaos and toward deliberate goals and outcomes. Therefore, our movement toward the CCSS is informed by the NCTE principles about what makes for strong ELA instruction and learning. With these principles in mind, we enact teaching practices that invite students to learn in ways that will enable them to meet the CCSS. The relationship between teaching and learning practices is key. Our teaching opens the space and makes explicit for students how they can learn to take up particular tasks and to ultimately take on particular dispositions toward lifelong learning.

Therefore, the following charts highlight some of the key NCTE principles about and teaching practices for reading instruction that the teachers in this chapter's vignettes connect to specific Reading Anchor Standards in the CCSS document, merging how the two teachers expect students to evidence their ability to enact the standards in their learning.

**Common Core Standards That Intersect with These Practices**

**Reading Standards for Literature, Grades 6–8**
10. By the end of the year, read and comprehend literature, including stories, dramas, and poems, in the grades 6–8 text complexity band proficiently, with scaffolding as needed at the high end of the range.

**Writing Standards, Grades 6–8**
1. Write arguments to support claims with clear reasons and relevant audience.

| How Kathleen enacts the practice ↓ | ← Teaching Practice → | How Rod enacts the practice ↓ |
|---|---|---|
| → Requires students to keep a list of books that they have read to share with one another.<br>→ Encourages students to read books on their reading level to gain ideas for their own writing.<br>→ Uses journal entries and reflections to encourage the students to think critically about their own writing. | The teacher conducts mini-lessons about writing craft and conventions that students are expected to apply.<br><br>The teacher offers students choice of texts and topics, providing guidance while encouraging students to guide their own learning. | → Encourages students to think about the audience for their persuasive writing.<br>→ Uses real-world audiences to allow students to practice their persuasive writing through letter writing. |
| **How Kathleen's students enact the practice** ↓ | ← Learning Practice → | **How Rod's students enact the practice** ↓ |
| → Students try out ideas, experiment with craft, and practice using conventions by writing in writer's notebooks.<br>→ Students choose their own writing tasks and select their own books for independent reading with guidance and support from the teacher, who ensures students are being appropriately challenged. | Students choose substantial texts within their reading level to discuss with classmates and the teacher.<br><br>Students learn about persuasive writing through engagement in multiple genres including critical reflection, journal entries, and letter writing. | → Students write for authentic purposes to real audiences about issues of concern to themselves and their communities.<br>→ Students develop critical thinking as they investigate, discuss, and write about real-world issues. |

**NCTE Principles**

Students have daily opportunities to read books of their own choice in school.
Students have daily opportunities to write on topics of their own choice in school.
Literate practices are embedded in complex social practices.

*See pages 102–103 for more on NCTE principles regarding reading instruction and pages 104–105 for more on NCTE principles regarding writing instruction.*

## Common Core Standards That Intersect with These Practices

**Writing Standards, Grades 6–8**
5. With some guidance and support from peers and adults, develop and strengthen writing as needed by planning, revising, editing, rewriting, or trying a new approach.

**Speaking and Listening Standards, Grade 7**
5. Include multimedia components (e.g., graphics, images, music, sound) and visual displays in presentations to clarify information.

| How Kathleen enacts the practice | ← Teaching Practice → | How Rod enacts the practice |
|---|---|---|
| → Allows parents into the classroom and informs them regularly about their children's progress.<br>→ Uses an Elmo visual presenter to show examples of common grammar confusion in students' writing. | The teacher forges strong home–school and home–community connections to engage students and foster support for students' learning.<br><br>The teacher uses visual tools to teach writing skills to students with different learning styles. | → Uses a Photo Journal unit and YouTube clips to offer visual learning and increased connection to the outside world.<br>→ Allows students to pair-share written responses and discuss journal entries. |
| **How Kathleen's students enact the practice** | **← Learning Practice →** | **How Rod's students enact the practice** |
| → Students are open to and excited about sharing their work with family and peers. | Students utilize the support of home communities and peer communities in their projects and writing. | → Students are given opportunities to share, reflect, critique, and revisit a piece of writing through conversation with their peers. |

### NCTE Principles
Writing instruction must take into account that a good deal of workplace writing and other writing takes place in collaborative situations.
Writing instruction must include ample in-class and out-of-class opportunities for writing and should include writing for a variety of purposes and audiences.

*See pages 104–105 for more on NCTE principles regarding writing instruction and pages 106–107 for more on NCTE principles regarding speaking and listening.*

## Frames That Build: Exercises to Interpret the CCSS

The following are some exercises that may help you to individually or as a team work to interpret the CCSS in a way that makes sense for your teaching context.

- *Reading the standards.* Looking at the language of the CCSS, consider how you can integrate meaningful community-action projects into the curriculum that involve both reading and writing and meet standards across multiple strands.

- *Involving the community.* Both Kathleen and Rod illustrate the importance of involving parents and the surrounding community in instruction, whether that is a simple letter home or an extensive project involving multiple community members. When it comes to understanding how the CCSS will affect student learning in your specific context, you might consider involving community members in conversations about curriculum, in the curriculum itself, or in conversations surrounding the implications of the CCSS and their subsequent assessments for students in your area.

# Thinking Deeply about Text

# 3

Getting students to think about reading closely is an important skill. This type of thinking requires attention to details, understanding of inferences, audience awareness, character perspective, and language awareness. When the group of middle school teachers and I met, we discussed the challenge of teaching students to read text deeply. We reminisced about our own experiences in middle school literature classes in which we were instructed to read the stories and answer the questions—a technique that does not work well for the twenty-first-century middle schooler. Today's students, and perhaps even yesterday's pupils, need explicit instruction about reading, an opportunity to practice the skill, talk about the work, and apply the skill in a different context. Both Mary and Claire taught students using *The Outsiders* with different creative, active strategies to engage the young adolescents.

## Meet Mary James, Bumpus Middle School

Mary, a National Board Certified Teacher since 2004, is a seasoned educator of seventeen years who teaches eighth-grade reading and English language arts at Bumpus Middle School in Hoover, Alabama, a large suburb outside of Birmingham with a growing diverse population. It is the sixth largest city in the state with 73,000 residents, 13,000 students, and seventeen schools. About 16 percent of the student population qualifies for free or reduced-price lunch. When you talk to Mary about her teaching experience, you quickly learn of her passion for the profession and dedication to all of her students. She refers to all of them as "my students" with

**Connections**

For more ideas about ways you can engage in professional development both within and outside your school as Mary does, visit Chapter 6 of this volume.

pride, even the ones who have graduated. She takes such pride in each one, because to teach them, she has invested much time and energy learning how to be a more effective educator. Because of her personal commitment to professional development, Mary serves as a district leader in differentiated instruction. She has created a professional network for herself through conversations with a range of colleagues, from those who are beginning their careers to those who are enhancing their teaching of writing to those who are preparing to demonstrate a new level of mastery in the classroom. She works with preservice teachers, Red Mountain Writing Project participants, and candidates who seek National Board Certification. Conversations with all of these teachers contribute to the professional network Mary has created for herself. Dedicated to professional growth, she sees herself as a learner who constantly challenges herself to be a better teacher for all of her students.

Mary's school is currently eleven years old, the third middle school in the district, which houses more than 1,000 students during the regular school day. The average class size is twenty to twenty-five students and classes meet for forty-eight minutes. The school consists of a diverse population of students (56 percent Euro-American, 29 percent African American, 11 percent Pacific Islander, 3 percent other minority groups). About 20 percent of students are eligible for free or reduced-price lunch. Most classes in this school have a heterogeneous mix of students including children with special needs, English language learners, gifted students, and regular students. Mary's primary goal is for her students to develop an inner voice as they actively read. Mary explains to her students the thinking of a proficient reader. As one reads, often a "voice in your head" will speak in response to the text. Mary asks students to honor that voice instead of ignoring it. If the voice seems confused or has a strong emotional response to a passage, she teaches the students to use that inner voice to help understand text. This will promote critical thinking and questioning of texts, audiences, and sources of information.

### Importance of Inferring: Mary's Classroom

Mary designs units and lessons for her students to develop their critical thinking skills while, at the same time, expanding their understanding of the world around them as they become participants in decision making and lifelong learning. Using literature, Mary teaches students to ask questions about what they read and dig deeply for evidence implied in the text. She believes that this kind of careful reading can help them make choices about how they will share their learning through writing. For this class she engages students in searching for textual support for their claims about character development in *The Outsiders*.

At the beginning of class, Mary often connects the reading for the day to the previous readings by engaging students in activities that build on their prior knowledge. One of her bell ringer activities is "Quotes I Like," which requires the students to select and write striking quotes from the previous day's reading. Students choose the quotes and are given opportunities to explain the relationship to the text as a review of the previous day's reading and the relationship to their own lives, if applicable. One from *The Outsiders* that reoccurs several times in the discussion is "Things are rough all over."

After students review the previous day's reading, Mary transitions into discussing the next chapter's emerging theme. To help students focus their thinking for the day, Mary uses a focus strategy called "Investigative Literary Theme." This strategy gives the students a "theme" to think deeply about while they read the text, providing a focus for the reading. This phase, sometimes referred to as the "into" reading phase, gives students the opportunity to investigate a topic using their prior knowledge as a starting point to predict and make inferences before reading the text (Hirai et al., 83). Mary has learned over the years that students stay more active in the reading process when they have something to think about and process, not just recall or identify. For this lesson, she challenges students to think about the theme of "family" as it relates to the characters in the text. This gives the students a focus as they read. She explains that the reading for the day may challenge the traditional definition of family and the roles in the family. In addition, the reading focus for the day involves finding inferences in text to support the idea of family from multiple characters' perspectives. Mary asks students to consider the following: What is a family? How do the gangs resemble a family? How do they differ? Can a gang take the place of family?

To find information from the text about "family," Mary explains that the evidence may be implied in the text instead of explicitly stated. She conducts a five-minute mini-discussion on inferences in reading, sharing how readers can draw inferences from reading to learn more about the character. During the class, she reads a passage that implies that 16-year-old Sodapop is going to be a father. The students were surprised ("I didn't know Soda was like that!"), but this further explains how drawing inferences in reading can be important to understanding a message. Mary then uses another quote from the text as an example: "If I see you in the hall at school and don't speak, don't hold it against me." The students process what is implied about the character from the short statement.

**Common Core State Standards**

Mary asks students to choose a quote to analyze as a way to review text. This engages students directly with the text and gives them practice finding evidence to support their opinions and arguments.

**Common Core State Standards**

One of the reading standards for literature requires that students engage in critical examination of textual themes. Mary helps students critique theme in the text and analyze its development in the text by providing a theme for students to examine that day. As students gain proficiency and independence, they will be able to identify themes on their own.

**Connections**

Mary scaffolds student learning by first providing students with information about making inferences, then modeling the practice, and finally asking students to engage in the practice themselves. For more information on ways to scaffold instruction and curriculum, see Section III.

To apply this mini-discussion to the reading for the day, Mary uses Silent Graffiti to capture what the students infer from their close reading of text. Teaching this strategy explicitly helps students understand how to look at text to find evidence. Procedural knowledge, or the awareness of how to implement a strategy, helps students read text (Jetton and Dole 167). Mary adheres large chart paper to the walls. Each sheet has a novel character's name written on it. During the reading of the text, students are allowed to write on the paper an inference they draw from the text that tells them more about the character's development. Students write direct quotes (textual support), providing the page number for reference (optional). As a recording of the book is playing, students silently "popcorn" to the character's graffiti chart that corresponds to the quote they want to write. When Mary implements the popcorn strategy, she expects students to get out of their seats to write their quotes without teacher permission and to work respectfully and silently as they implement the strategy. Students appreciated the freedom to write their thinking without pressure from the teacher and to think carefully about their contributions to the class. The following are a few of the quotes the students wrote on the class graffiti charts:

**Common Core State Standards**

Students write comments about characters from multiple points of view. For example, quotes from Johnny about Dally may vary from the quotes selected from Soc Bob about Dally. This enables students learn to see a character as dynamic.

For Dally: "You get hardened in jail. I don't want it to happen to you like it happened to me."

For Ponyboy: "Greaser don't have nothing to do with it." Student response to the quote: "Being a Greaser has nothing to do with who you are."

For Ponyboy: "He is not a Soc, he is just a guy."

Students compile a list of quotes and responses from the text to discuss the development of each of the characters in the text. This strategy is the building block for a literary analysis paper that students will write after they finish reading the book. The long-term goal for this explicit strategy instruction is for students to transfer the learning to "conditional knowledge" (Jetton and Dole 167), the ability of students to use the strategy in other contexts, depending on the situation and the textual needs of the reader.

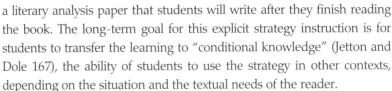

**Connections**

Mary emphasizes the importance of active learning in class through constant monitoring of student learning. For more information on formative assessment and ways to incorporate it into your teaching and curriculum, see Section III.

In addition to the graffiti pages that students create during class, Mary keeps two charts hanging in her classroom the whole time students are reading *The Outsiders*: an "I think" chart and an "I wonder" chart. Students add to these pages as they continue with the book, writing statements and questions such as "Will Ponyboy fight in the rumble?" and "Randy could be suicidal [because of the death of best friend Bob]." Strategies such as graffiti pages and the two charts allow students a space to write their thoughts as they respond to the text throughout the unit. Students write on the charts sporadically during the unit.

Mary stops the tape in seven- to ten-minute intervals to check student comprehension and analysis. Instead of asking basic recall questions, she starts with open-ended questions that challenge students to find support from the text. Questioning students during the reading of the text helps them process as they read, instead of after they read. The types of questions teachers ask students shape the discussion; teachers control the dynamics of the class through the types of questions with which they decide to engage students. To begin the class discussion, Mary asks, "What did we learn about family?" and "What gave us that impression?" Students begin to talk about how the Greasers took care of each other in the absence of the traditional family structure. One student adds, "They have nothing to lose," referring to the protective family structure that emerges from the Greasers. Students then begin to compare and contrast their own families to the ones in the text. Mary builds on their discussion with an end-of-class activity designed to help students summarize the discussion for themselves. To end the class, Mary uses the Literary Processing Card that asks students to respond to one of two questions related to the reading: (1) Do teenagers really want limits? and (2) Should parents force students to accept responsibility for their actions? Students write their responses on these cards as they leave the classroom. This "through" reading strategy assesses the students' learning and helps Mary develop plans the following day related to students' understanding. Students still process their learning as they walk to the door. One student says to another, "You have the wrong idea about Soda." She responds, "Naw, I think I know his type exactly." The discussion trails into the hallway.

## Active Teacher, Active Learner: Mary's Journey

Mary describes her journey as one that has been directed by the students' needs. Having taught in different educational situations (low poverty, high income, culturally diverse, culturally homogeneous, high needs, etc.), she has learned much from her students, especially students she instructed early in her career who were struggling readers in secondary school. When Mary started her teaching career, she believed that older students would engage in and be capable of conversations about literature at high levels. What she learned quickly was that not all or even most students, in fact, were extremely interested in daily lectures or canonical literature, especially when they had no connection to the people or the time period. A little discouraged, Mary began to talk honestly to her students about what they wanted from school and the best way to accomplish the goal.

> **Integrated Teaching and Learning**
>
> Mary learned quickly that to meet the needs of her students, she would need to take on the role of a learner and let them communicate their needs. This allowed her to learn both about her students and about herself as a teacher. Consider what you do to learn more about your students. What else could you do?

She used techniques and strategies (reading inventories, journals, interest surveys, questionnaires, writing responses) that allowed her to know more about her students and, in turn, more about herself as a teacher. It was then that she realized the importance of teaching students as individuals and building relationships to help instruct them more effectively. She says, "My students teach me how to teach."

She takes the information she learns continuously from students and incorporates it into her lesson design. Mary relies heavily on professional development to assist her with creating and implementing a curriculum that allows her students to be the most successful. As a member of several formal and informal learning communities, she uses resources from NCTE, the National Writing Project, the National Board of Professional Teaching Standards, National Middle School Association, and online resources to assist her in her planning. One current area of inquiry for her is teaching English language learners in the mainstream classroom. As she has done in the past, she begins by getting to know her non-English-speaking students better, even when conversations consist mostly of gestures and pictures. She and her teammates construct plans that will meet the needs of the English language learners, and at the same time, Mary consults with national networks of teachers for professional development in this area, participating in NCTE's Connected Community and the National Writing Project interactive site.

**Connections**

For more ideas about professional development opportunities and lesson planning resources, see Section III and Appendix A.

**Web 3.1**

Mary integrates into her instruction the information she gathers about how students learn, using it to develop differentiated instruction within her class. She carefully designs lessons that differ in process, product, and/or content. For example, the culminating activity for *The Outsiders* allows students to choose if they want to work with a partner or alone. By giving students this choice, she accommodates varying learning styles and abilities. Her comparison/contrast project offers students four choices: an analytical Venn diagram comparing and contrasting two groups within a theme with textual support; a self-designed chart that demonstrates understanding of a key theme in the text related to the similarities and differences of major characters; an expository essay written for a real audience about a teacher-approved aspect of the text (e.g., pros and cons of the role of social service in the text vs. society); or a symbolic shield representation of each of the groups in the text with a short synopsis describing the similarities and differences illustrated on the shields. Students also prepare for Socratic seminar discussions during the unit. Students lead and research the Seminar discussion topics developed from their inquiry question about the text. All students participate in the lively discussions led by their peers as Mary facilitates and monitors the learning they demonstrate.

**Honoring Diversity**

Mary allows students a lot of choices about what topics they will examine, how they will lead discussions about that topic, and how they will present their topic to their classmates. Student choice, when well facilitated and guided by the teacher, is a great way to honor students' differences and differentiate instruction.

Mary provides multiple opportunities for student success during instruction as well as during the assessment phase. She believes that students are individuals who have multiple ways of absorbing, seeing, and analyzing their worlds, so in addition to the traditional paper-and-pencil quizzes, she relies heavily on alternative assessments for students to incorporate their learning at higher levels. Throughout the unit on *The Outsiders,* she used students' response to literature, Silent Graffiti writing, literary analysis, class discussions, and Socratic seminars to gauge student learning. Mary sums up her approach to teaching:

> I want my students to know that I care about their learning. I carefully design lessons that will help them be successful, but I do not sacrifice rigor; I actually increase it. I give them opportunities to take control of the learning process. When they have choices, their buy-in is greater, their response is healthier, their learning is more authentic. I want my students to be lifelong learners who can think and process different types of text. If I can do all of this, I think I have given them a solid foundation in the ELA classroom.

## Meet Claire Hardin, Phillips Academy K–8

Claire is a seventh-grade reading and English language arts teacher in urban Birmingham, Alabama. The school system has approximately 25,000 students, with roughly 85 percent of the population qualifying for free and reduced-price lunch. Claire has been teaching for five years in the district and for three years at her present school. Her short professional career has included a mixture of challenges and successes in the profession. Claire admits that she always had a thirst to learn more about teaching, but sometimes her initial teaching practices did not provide for effective student learning. Students rarely turned homework in, they seemed distant from the learning process, and they did not readily accept the innovative strategies she used in class. When she expressed frustration, Claire's mentor teacher shared this observation:

> You have excellent ideas, but you are trying too much, too early, too quickly without a viable plan for the students you teach. Many of your students are used to teacher-centered instruction, and you must

teach them how to take more responsibility for their learning . . . gradually. Your ideas are wonderful, but you cannot do everything at once. You must remember to teach the children, not just the content.

Claire took this advice to heart. She began to examine closely her population of students. She learned that 94 percent of her students were living in poverty, and many of their families were unable to spend much time supporting student learning at home. With this in mind, Claire began to evaluate what she was teaching and how she was teaching it. She realized painfully that she was covering the content but not reaching the students. Claire, as a new teacher to the profession, began to make gradual changes to her class, responding directly to her students' learning needs.

Now, four years later, Claire's teaching practice has changed dramatically. Her present building, a preK–8 magnet school, serves a student body that is 98 percent African American, 1 percent Asian, and 1 percent Hispanic. About 52 percent of the students qualify for free or reduced-price lunch. In the early grades, most of those enrolled are students zoned for Claire's school; however, the middle school students apply to attend. For this reason, most of Claire's seventh-grade students are academically gifted students who were chosen from throughout the urban school district.

This facility is an old one that started as a high school and now has been renovated to accommodate grades K–8. Filled with history, the building has large columns and majestic front doors that open to more than 600 students each day. The average middle school class size ranges from twenty-four to twenty-eight students, and classes meet for fifty minutes. The classes are heterogeneously grouped, putting together English language learners, gifted students, and regular education students. However, the selection process involved with being a magnet school makes the student population less diverse by ability.

## Using Visual Art and Literature: Claire's Classroom

**Honoring Diversity**

Claire displays student work to give students additional audiences other than the teacher. This honors the voices students bring to the classroom and fosters a supportive environment in Claire's diverse school setting.

Claire's classroom has student work on every wall, file cabinet, and available unused space on the floor. The entire space feels like a student-centered learning environment, rich with different types of texts created by students. This day, all of the desks are pushed close to the wall, making room for all twenty-eight students to work on the floor. Claire says that by the end of a unit, she wants students to take ownership of their learning through art and close reading.

Over the last four years, Claire has learned more about creating effective curriculum and implementing it strategically. She has focused on scaffolding meaningful and purposeful steps that lead to rigorous learning experiences for the students. She uses *The Outsiders* as the text to accomplish this during the second nine weeks of the year. She believes the themes, characters, and plot development of this text engage students, while at the same time teaching them to analyze the literature critically, seeing pieces of themselves through the characters. To accomplish this, Claire begins with the end in mind. She decides what she wants student to know by the end of the unit and creates "baby steps" to achieve that goal. For this unit, she wanted students to understand the importance of textual information (facts) to support claims (opinions).

**Common Core State Standards**
Like Mary, Claire engages her students in activities that will help them find evidence to support their ideas, a skill they will build on in their writing.

Claire culminates her unit using the Postmortem of a Protagonist group activity. Using art in literature, she engages students who enjoy visual arts learning activities, creating a responsive classroom environment that is also inclusive of students' extracurricular literacies (National Council of Teachers of English 3). Several 6' by 3' sheets of colorful paper line the wooden floor. Sprawled on one large sheet of construction paper, a student lies still as Claire traces her body outline. Modeling the learning activity, Claire explains that it is important for the one who draws to be careful outlining the volunteer "corpse" because the artist should not soil the corpse's clothes with marker or trace in disrespectful body spaces. The student, the corpse model, remains still during the demonstration, moving quickly after the body drawing is complete. Claire then assigns a major character from the book to each group of four, then assigning body parts that she wants "textually examined" using note cards. Each note card will include quotations and passages from the text to support claims about students' thoughts about a character, a "textual autopsy." For example, Claire asks students to examine Johnny's eyes in literal and figurative language with textual support.

Students work in groups to design their postmortem character. Seven groups of students work on the floor making decisions about the characters' appearances and internal struggles. Claire allows the groups to grapple with this on two levels: roles/responsibilities as group members and discussion about relevant content. During class, she facilitates the learning, rotating from group to group. Students use the self-directed learning activity as a way to express their understanding of the character's role in the text. One group decides to divide a character in half, arguing that he had split roles in the book; sometimes he was a positive character when associating with a few characters, but other times he was hard and negative toward others. Students ask questions of each other about the appearance of the character as they search for textual support.

**Integrated Teaching and Learning**
Students become active learners in their learning process. The teacher facilitates, but students make choices about how they will complete tasks. In this way, students learn to teach themselves and one another how they best learn, with the teacher's guidance.

To prepare for the autopsy, Claire designs instruction teaching students to use text to support claims. Two key strategies help students develop an understanding of fact and opinion. One is the creation of T-charts as students read the texts. On one side of the chart, students write what characters actually do (actions); on the other side, students write what the actions mean (inferences). This type of double-entry writing allows students to understand that actions have meaning, even if this is not explicitly stated. The second teaching strategy is Silent Conversation. Divided into small groups, each student receives a paper that has a space for a quote, question, and response. Each student finds five quotes that affect his or her thinking about a character or the text and writes a question about each quote. The paper is then passed to the next group member, who responds to one of the quotes and questions. The students continue to pass their papers to gather responses from all group members. When the paper returns to the writer, the student can respond to the input gained from classmates or open the discussion for further input. This silent writing activity helps students process their thinking before discussing it, and at the same time it helps them look more carefully at the text.

Claire also uses a Venn diagram activity for students to compare and contrast different groups and characters from the text. In one diagram, a student compares and contrasts Socs and Greasers, citing primary transportation differences: cars and trucks vs. bicycles and walking. In another diagram that compares and contrasts Cliques and Gangs, a student writes, "both include a group of friends who have something in common that binds them." Claire wanted students to understand the contrasts and similarities that exist between the two groups. Her overall goal was for students to recognize that, despite obvious differences, people can come together based on common similarities that connect us as humankind.

Another strategy Claire uses to encourage careful attention to the text is the written Open Mic Wall. Instead of allowing students to talk about their responses to a generalized statement, Claire requires students to first write about their responses. Students can then process their own thinking before sharing with the group. On a large poster board, Claire writes a statement in the center. Students then respond using prior knowledge unrelated to the text. Claire shows that she values the students' voices and perspective in this activity. At the same time, she can see misconceptions and perceptions that she will address during the study of the text. She can then bring in secondary reading that speaks to the needs of the students in a way that the main text may not. Newspaper articles about gangs, websites about foster care, blogs about stereotypes, and news clips about teen violence can illuminate the entire reading experience for students. Claire uses the Open Mic Wall to gauge students' thinking before official classroom discussion begins about the topic. One of the statements that students comment on is "A person is often stereotyped by the people he/she hangs out with." In response, students write comments like these:

- The people you hang out with could be backstabbers. [People will believe you are, too.]

- I disagree because it is wrong to judge. [People should not be tied to the company they keep.]

- Yes, because some of the people they hang out with may talk about people behind their back. [If the people you hang with talk about people, others will think you do, too.]

**Honoring Diversity**
Claire gives every student a chance to voice their ideas and uses these ideas to mold the rest of the unit, instead of walking in with a completely pre-planned unit. This allows her to meet the needs of her students and also enables her to gauge students' thinking early on and throughout the unit.

Another of Claire's assignments asks students to focus on descriptive writing that calls on their visual literacy. Students choose family pictures and instead of focusing on the story behind the picture, the students describe the event in the picture in detail using their senses, practicing their use of figurative language. Writing this way prepares students for the culminating activity that will require them to use rich vocabulary and thick description.

## Learning to Balance: Claire's Journey

Claire smiles when she looks back on her five years of teaching. In the beginning she felt overwhelmed:

> I had so many things coming at me at once. I had testing requirements for three different assessments. I had benchmark assessments. I had common assessments for my teaching team. I had tests and quizzes. I had remediation and gifted lessons. I had course of study standards, national standards, all kinds of standards. What I have learned, though, [is] that none of this makes any difference if I cannot organize my curriculum in meaningful ways for students. I could not keep throwing disconnected standards at them and expect that they could gain understanding beyond the surface levels. I had to find a way to make learning flow and build.

But the advice of her mentor to "teach the children, not just the content" and to avoid "trying too much, too early, too quickly" helped her develop greater awareness of her students' needs and incorporate individual standards into a larger curricular plan that is culturally responsive and developmentally appropriate for her students. When asked how she incorporates the CCSS into her practice, she calmly states that she looks at the standards and decides how they can add focus or new dimensions to her existing curriculum. If she finds that she is not addressing a particular standard, she will rethink her teaching to include the standard.

 **Collaboration**

Through collaboration, Claire finds support and new ideas to support her curriculum development and instruction. For more information about professional learning communities, visit ncte.org/books/supp-students-6-8.

She believes that she is able to incorporate the CCSS because she is a part of a strong professional development network at school and beyond. Her teaching team in the building is collaborative, always discussing ways to make instruction better for students as a whole. Her team is already positioned to discuss literacy in the content areas. In addition to this, Claire is an active member of the National Writing Project. She reads professional books and attends local professional development opportunities. All of these opportunities for working with her peers enable Claire to continue learning and growing as a teacher.

## Charting the Practices

Both of these vignettes illustrate how class lessons that work well include an integration of all literacy strands—reading, writing, speaking, listening, language, and viewing. Specifically, however, our two vignettes function as powerful examples of the importance of helping students develop visual literacies along with more traditional literacy practices such as reading and writing the printed word. The following charts show how these teachers address specific standards in the CCSS in concert with NCTE principles to shape their teaching practices. The charts also include the learning practices students are expected to exhibit in response to the teaching practices.

## Common Core Standards That Intersect with These Practices

**Speaking and Listening Standards, Grades 6–8**

1. Engage effectively in a range of collaborative discussions (one-on-one, in groups, and teacher-led) with diverse partners on grade-level topics, texts, and issues, building others' ideas, and expressing their own clearly.

| How Mary enacts the practice | ◄——— Teaching Practice ———► | How Claire enacts the practice |
|---|---|---|
| → Teaches summarizing strategies to help students connect each day's reading to previous chapters.<br>→ Provides students with a thematic framework to help them consider the text from multiple perspectives.<br>→ Gives students public space to share their thinking on "I think" and "I wonder" charts. | The teacher engages students in multiple cognitive strategies such as predicting, questioning, confirming, summarizing, and inferring to develop comprehension and critical thinking.<br><br>The teacher facilitates and guides students as they engage in discussion and deep thinking about texts. | → Provides multiple opportunities for students to investigate the text by talking, writing, drawing, and charting their interpretations of characters and events.<br>→ Builds students' inference skills by using a variety of strategies that give students practice in creating claims and finding supporting evidence in the text. |
| **How Mary's students enact the practice** | ◄——— Learning Practice ———► | **How Claire's students enact the practice** |
| → Students choose quotes from the reading as a way to review and analyze text.<br>→ Students make inferences about characters using textual evidence.<br>→ Students write about characters from multiple points of view; students learn to see a character as dynamic. | Guided by the teacher, students make choices about how they will complete tasks, becoming actively engaged in their learning processes.<br><br>Students support one another's learning through written and spoken conversations about text; speaking prepares them for writing and vice-versa. | → Students create T-charts as they read to capture actions and inferences.<br>→ Working in groups, students collaborate to create a "textual autopsy" of one of the main characters.<br>→ Students process their thinking on an Open Mic Wall before sharing their ideas with the group. |

### NCTE Principles
In discussions of texts, teachers should welcome multiple perspectives, themes, and interpretations.

*See pages 106–107 for more on NCTE principles regarding speaking and listening.*

**Common Core Standards That Intersect with These Practices**

**Reading Standards for Literature, Grades 6–8**
1. Cite textual evidence to support analysis of what the text says explicitly as well as inferences drawn from the text.
2. Determine a theme or central idea of a text and how it is conveyed through particular details; provide a summary of the text distinct from personal opinions or judgments.

| How Mary enacts the practice | ← Teaching Practice → | How Claire enacts the practice |
|---|---|---|
| → Uses direct quotations within the text to encourage students to dig more deeply for evidence.<br>→ Gives students a specific and relevant theme within the literature to think about and discuss. | Teachers enable students to read literature closely by using a focus strategy to give students a theme to think about while reading the text.<br><br>Teachers teach textual analysis by asking students to make inferences about specific quotations, which they generate based on their reading of the literature. | → Uses themes, characters, and plot development to engage students in the literature.<br>→ Encourages students to use direct quotations to support their claims about characters.<br>→ Uses T-charts and Silent Conversation to allow students to practice creating their own claims and finding supporting inferences in the text. |
| How Mary's students enact the practice | ← Learning Practice → | How Claire's students enact the practice |
| → Students write direct quotes from the text for textual support about a character's development.<br>→ Students consider a specific theme within a text and discuss this theme with the class. | Students think deeply about a particular theme as they read, providing a focus for their reading.<br><br>Students pick out quotes as textual support to understand theme and character development. | → Students participate in several exercises to practice critical thinking and textual citation to explain character development.<br>→ Students become active learners and work to express their understanding of a character's role in the literature. |

**NCTE Principles**
Teachers should provide regular opportunities for students to respond to reading through discussion, writing, art, drama, storytelling, music, and other creative expressions.
Teachers should provide specific feedback to students to support their reading development.

*See pages 102–103 for more on NCTE principles regarding reading instruction.*

## Frames That Build: Exercises to Interpret the CCSS

The following are a few exercises for individual or teams of teachers to use to work more with the standards and see how these vignettes may provide a lens through which to view your own interpretation and individualized implementation of the standards.

- *Reading the standards.* Individually or with a group of teachers, examine the reading standards across the middle school grade levels and identify the language related to student thought during reading. Consider how your current curriculum engages students in "deep thinking about texts" and share ways you might address the demands of the reading standards.
- *Weighing classroom decisions.* Consider how the exercises in which Mary and Claire engage their students—finding direct quotes from texts and sharing them to support their claims and ideas—might continue to transfer into students' writing practices. Look at the CCSS and at your curriculum for places where you can integrate reading, writing, speaking, and listening. Discuss meaningful ways to "layer" multiple literacy tasks with your colleagues and share ideas.

# 4

# Reading/Writing Workshop

*W*orkshop is a term that has taken on many different meanings, and it is enacted in a variety of ways by individual teachers. As the two vignettes below demonstrate, even when teachers are using the same text in a workshop context, their classes can look very different. This is a good thing. The flexibility of reading/writing workshop means that teachers can adapt it to the specific context in which they work, addressing individual student needs as well as school and district requirements. At the same time, central features of workshop make it an excellent way to address the CCSS. The integration of reading, writing, speaking, listening, and language can be accomplished effectively in reading/writing workshop. This is also an approach that encourages active and independent learning as well as transfer of learning—all attributes that the CCSS emphasize for students.

## Meet Rick Joseph, Covington School

Covington School, where Rick Joseph teaches, is located in an affluent suburb of Detroit where the per capita income is one of the highest in the nation. This is reflected in the student population, where less than 5 percent is eligible for free or reduced-price lunch. Covington serves 648 students in grades 3–8, with twenty-seven youngsters in each class. Students are 88 percent Euro-American, 6 percent African American, 5 percent Asian, and 1 percent Latino or other. Many parents are actively involved in the school, providing material resources via PTA funding and human resources of time and talent. Teachers can request budgets for special projects from the PTA, and it is common for parents to visit class to share ideas and activities from their professions. In addition to traditional teaching materials, the school provides a technology-rich environment so that Rick can integrate the digital world into his classroom. Both computer labs and laptop carts are available to students.

The school also supports professional development with weekly team planning time and monthly half-day team planning time focused on technology integration. Parent involvement in students' education is high, so one of the challenges of teaching in a school like Covington, Rick explains, is educating parents so that they understand what he is trying to accomplish in his classes.

Rick is in his sixteenth year of teaching and his seventh year at Covington. He taught for nine years in Chicago in three different schools, all serving a majority of Latino students. Fluent in Spanish, Rick became a teacher because he wanted to address the achievement gap between European American and Latino students, and he chose to work in urban schools where the need was greatest. From early in his career, collaborating with other teachers has been important to Rick. He learns from sharing ideas with colleagues, exploring together the challenges and questions that arise in classrooms. Working toward certification by the National Board for Professional Teaching Standards (NBPTS) pushed him to examine his teaching practices closely, and at the same time it provided him opportunities to learn from colleagues. Likewise, being on a design team for the National Teachers' Academy, serving as a mentor teacher at the Chicago Academy, and participating in the Academy for Urban School Leadership have all contributed to Rick's growth as a teacher. In each of these contexts he has enhanced his own teaching practice by working with colleagues.

Since moving to Michigan, Rick has been active with the National Writing Project and with the Network of Michigan Educators. Both of these experiences have deepened Rick's thinking about the most effective ways to develop students' abilities as readers and writers. "I can't imagine being a teacher without having opportunities to work with colleagues," he claims. He comes to his 5/6 multi-age classroom, where he teaches both English and social studies, energized and ready to provide rich learning experiences for his students. These learning experiences extend outside the classroom, as Rick teaches an after-school class in video production.

In every teaching context Rick's goals are the same: to help all his students become lifelong readers and writers, to read actively and compose creatively by choice, to use their skills to help others in real and meaningful ways, and to make significant academic growth from wherever they are to wherever they can possibly go.

## Workshop with New Media: Rick's Classroom

"Welcome to Reader's Workshop" is on the screen when students walk into Rick's sixth-grade classroom on a sunny November day. Students sit in teams at tables, and their pictures are on the wall surrounded by character traits with which they have identified. On the "We Are Geniuses!" bulletin board students have put their names under the type of intelligence they prefer, reflecting their understanding of multiple intelligences. A Battle of the Books bulletin board lists students' reading progress. Students have brought in pictures, mainly of parents, for the "Who Are Your Mentors?" bulletin board.

As soon as students are settled, Rick puts the lyrics to "Sweet Home Alabama" on the screen, asking if they recognize it. They identify it as a popular Kid Rock song, and Rick explains that it originated with a band called Lynyrd Skynyrd. Then he points to the lyrics about returning to Alabama "to see my kin," and he notes that the Watsons, of *The Watsons Go to Birmingham—1963,* are going to Alabama to visit family. Then he asks the team captains to distribute books and thinkmarks to their teams.

**Common Core State Standards**

Rick integrates language instruction with reading instruction, meeting multiple standards and incorporating different types of literacy knowledge into a single lesson plan.

"What is dialogue?" Rick asks. He demonstrates a dialogue with a student and identifies the prefix *di-* as meaning two. Then he asks, "How do you know when dialogue is good?" One student says that good dialogue has to include questions. When some students disagree, Rick asks two volunteers to try to have a conversation without questions and then asks them how it felt. Rick types and projects their responses on the screen for the class to consider.

Rick reads aloud a section of dialogue from page 35 of *The Watsons,* using character voices, and then asks students to discuss in pairs whether this is good dialogue. Students talk for about two minutes while Rick walks around listening in, then he reports some of what he has heard about the nature of good dialogue. He mentions terms such as *realistic, appropriate word choice,* and *fast paced* and asks students if they had similar thoughts. They indicate by raising their hands that they did.

Next Rick projects Independent Reading Instructions:

1. Read from wherever you left off.

2. Focus on author Christopher Paul Curtis's use of dialogue.

3. As you find good use of dialogue, note the page number and explain why on your thinkmark.

**Connections**

Formative assessment happens all the time in the classroom as teachers formally and informally conduct "checks" to see what students understand and have learned. Rick conducts formative evaluation of individual students, recording their progress in reading. For more information about formative assessments, see Section I.

4. Try for at least two examples of dialogue in your reading today.

5. We will stop at 10:45.

As students read and record examples of good dialogue on their thinkmarks, Rick conferences individually with four to five students, asking them questions about the text ("Who do you like better: Kenny or Byron?") and asking them to read a portion of the text aloud to promote support for their preferences. This strategy also gives him a way to monitor students' reading abilities. Rick makes notes about their reading on a grid chart on his laptop.

Rick tilts a rainstick to end independent reading. Then he shows a model wiki response to this journal assignment, explaining that students will be making wiki entries, too. He demonstrates that a successful entry will cite the page number, describe what is happening in the book, give "my ideas," and tell how the dialogue is effective. He goes on to explain that dialogue on a wiki and face-to-face dialogue follow similar rules.

Students then turn to face one another and discuss the good dialogue they found. Rick asks one pair to share with the class what they discussed, after he and a student volunteer have modeled how to cite page numbers and read with their partner from the book. When students read passages that aren't dialogue, Rick shows students how quotation marks and other punctuation can help them identify dialogue. Team captains collect the books, and Rick plays a few seconds of "Sweet Home Alabama" as students leave.

**Common Core State Standards**

In this discussion about dialogue, Rick draws his students' attention to different types of texts and text structures. This instruction will help students when they confront texts with different conventions, which is required by the CCSS and common in today's English classrooms.

## *Growing in Professional Learning Communities: Rick's Journey*

Rick has been using a workshop approach to teaching for a number of years, but he didn't use it in his first years of teaching. It was something he grew into as he became more experienced. After he had completed his MA and was regularly getting good evaluations for his classroom work, it would have been easy for him to coast, but, as he puts it, "I wanted to improve and become an even better teacher." Preparing for NBPTS certification gave him an opportunity to meet with a group of colleagues who analyzed their own teaching as well as the work done by their students. He explains, "I needed a supportive community and positive peer pressure. Left to my own devices, I fall into a rut and don't necessarily teach as effectively as I can when I know I will be sharing my practice."

Because of Rick's interest in motivating reluctant readers and writers, the workshop approach was especially attractive to him. He recognized that features of workshop such as peer interactions, opportunities for monitoring the learning of individual students, and sustained reading and writing would help him engage students who were not inherently drawn to literacy. Rick saw the value in using a workshop approach in his classes, but it was the sharing with colleagues that led him to implement it. Getting together regularly with other teachers to share ideas about instruction and student learning—a practice he continues into the present—helped him and still helps him take up the challenge of transforming his teaching practices. Whether the NBPTS cohort, the Academy for Urban School Leadership, or the Network of Michigan Educators in which he currently participates, professional learning communities have always been an important part of Rick's teaching. Covington's allocation of weekly and monthly team planning time gives Rick another professional learning community in which he

**Connections**

For more information on implementing a workshop approach in your classroom, consult the resources in Appendix A at the end of this volume.

can continue to grow as an educator and to share practice with other professionals in the building.

A workshop approach requires detailed knowledge about each student, and Rick starts the school year with three surveys—about reading, writing, and general interests—to get acquainted with his students, both personally and academically. Because he teaches in a multi-age setting, he has many of the same students for two years and gets to know them well. He also learns a lot from conversations with parents who, as he puts it, "have so much more longitudinal knowledge of their child's academic and social/emotional history."

Formative assessment is central to Rick's teaching. He regularly gathers information about students' responses to and comprehension of the literature they read and the quality of what they write. Asking individual students a few questions about their reading or having them read passages aloud, as he did in the vignette included here, gives him a clear indication about their comprehension of the text and this, in turn, enables him to modify his teaching to help them learn. Rather than waiting for a test at the end of the unit, Rick is able to assess student learning on a regular basis, and the notes he keeps on each student help him chart progress.

When Rick looks at the CCSS he sees connections with many of his own goals. In harmony with the CCSS Anchor Standards for reading, he wants his students to read closely and cite evidence from the text, discern central ideas, analyze the development of ideas, interpret the language of texts, analyze textual structures, assess point of view, evaluate content in diverse media, evaluate arguments, analyze thematic similarities, and read independently and proficiently. He also knows that students need to be engaged and motivated to accomplish these things, and he works hard to connect with their interests—such as the song in the vignette—and to affirm them as learners—as the bulletin boards in his room show—so that they will become lively participants in their own learning.

**Common Core State Standards**

Rick examined the CCSS for standards that speak to similar goals as those he already held for his students. Try reading the CCSS with an eye toward where your goals and the goals of the standards are particularly "in harmony" with one another. Use these places to reflect on ways you can integrate the standards into your existing curriculum, and consider how and where to adjust your curriculum. For more ideas about curriculum planning, see Section III.

The CCSS Anchor Standard that emphasizes using technology to produce and publish writing as well as interact and collaborate with others fits well with Rick's—and his school's—emphasis on technology integration. In keeping with this and with NCTE's definition of 21st century literacies, Rick wants his students to learn to work collaboratively, share information for a variety of purposes, analyze multiple streams of information, create and evaluate multimedia texts, and attend to the ethical responsibilities of digital environments. To this end he regularly integrates technology into his teaching, exposing students to a variety of texts, as was evident in the vignette. He also requires his students to produce new media texts, as his wiki assignment demonstrates.

Rick's journey has taken him to a variety of schools, and it has led him to work with many different kinds of students, but the desire to improve his practice has been constant in all of these settings and with all of his students. Collaboration with colleagues, both in his own school and from other schools, plays a key role in Rick's ongoing development as a teacher.

## Meet Sarah Rennick, Reuther Middle School

Sarah Rennick has been teaching for eleven years, but like all teachers who develop their practice year after year, she regularly takes up new approaches. During the past two years, she has begun using a workshop approach, and, as she puts it, her goal is "to get better at implementing it." Sarah's turn to the workshop approach was part of a school- and districtwide transformation that is part of the School Improvement Plan. Reuther Middle School, where Sarah teaches, is one of four middle schools in a suburban district that has a good record of student achievement. Overall, more than 80 percent of students in the district typically demonstrate proficiency on state-mandated tests.

This district has invested significant resources in the professional development of its teachers. Each grade level in each school has teacher leaders who meet regularly with one another to develop curriculum materials. Teachers receive release time to visit the classrooms of peers who are modeling specific teaching approaches. And a number of teachers have received support to participate in summer workshops to develop new teaching strategies. Three years ago, the school district developed a Teaching Checklist that includes both teaching strategies and specific content. For example, sixth-grade ELA teachers in the district are expected to help students learn about concepts such as point of view, summary, protagonist/antagonist, and metaphor. Teaching strategies for such concepts include brainstorming, using websites, writing riddles, and creating comic strips.

**Collaboration**

Sarah and her colleagues collaborate by sharing teaching responsibilities within a single grade level and co-planning workshop activities. For other ideas about ways in which you might collaborate with your colleagues, see Section III.

As a teacher leader, Sarah has been regularly involved in working with her colleagues to decide on the best strategies for fostering student learning. Reading/writing workshop was slated for adoption at the middle level after it had been successfully implemented in the district's elementary schools. After first beginning to implement workshop last year, Sarah decided that it would be easier to move into the process more slowly. Accordingly, she and her teaching partner have divided reading and writing workshops, with Sarah doing reading workshop one semester and writing the other. Working as a team, each of them sees all 120 sixth graders every other week. This way she is able to focus on one dimension at a time rather than plunging into the whole thing at once. Reading workshop requires students to read fifteen books (books with at least 150 pages) each year, 450 pages the first quarter, and 600 pages per quarter after that.

### Text to Text, Text to World: Sarah's Classroom

Colorful kites hang from the ceiling in Sarah's bright and cheerful classroom. Images of popular book covers are posted on the wall under a sign that says "Have You Read This?" and students sit in three rows of paired desks. A SMART Board, TV, teacher computer, and three student computers comprise the technological resources. When

**Common Core State Standards**

The CCSS call for students to be proficient readers of both informational and fictional texts; novels with historical references like those in *The Watsons Go to Birmingham* can be paired with nonfiction texts to both increase students' background knowledge and engage them with different types of texts on similar topics.

students come into the room, they turn in their reading logs, pick up their worksheets, and collect their journals and reading books. They three-hole punch their worksheets to put into their binders and then turn to the class's main text, *The Watsons Go to Birmingham,* which Sarah surrounds with other texts. For example, she shares material about the Civil Rights Movement; a 1963 article about the church bombing in Birmingham, Alabama; and an article about the recent death (in prison) of one of the convicted bombers. She incorporates texts like these because she wants her students to be able to connect their reading with the larger world. Sarah passes out new reading logs and reminds students that they need to include a one-sentence summary for each of their twenty-minute readings—a total of 220 minutes by November 23. The guidelines are clear, but students need to take responsibility for accomplishing the specified amount of reading.

Sarah begins by showing a PowerPoint presentation on character types, encouraging her students to distinguish between protagonists and antagonists. She gives a definition of each and then asks students to talk with one another about which character in *The Watsons* fits these definitions. Then she does the same thing with round, flat, static, and dynamic characters. When students have difficulty deciding, Sarah offers more information. For example, when they wonder if Joey is a round character, she explains that they should be able to name five characteristics of a round character. Her goal is to give students language that they can use in discussing the book, language that can be transferred to other discussions and other English classes.

Sarah then reads aloud a portion of Chapter 9 from *The Watsons* where Kenny and his father have a heart-to-heart conversation about why Byron, Kenny's older brother, is going to spend some time with his grandmother in Alabama instead of remaining with the rest of the family in Michigan. She asks students to turn and talk with a peer about a time when they participated in a conversation where parents treated them as if they were adults. Students talk animatedly with one another, and Sarah moves around the room, listening to them. This conversation gives students an opportunity to think more deeply about the text and at the same time to make connections between it and their own experiences.

After this discussion, Sarah asks students to write in their journals in response to these questions: Who is the protagonist/antagonist in your independent reading? Why? In explaining the journal writing assignment, Sarah reminds students of the PowerPoint presentation she used at the beginning of class. By asking students to use terms she just introduced, Sarah creates a connection between in-class reading and the reading students are doing independently. In addition, this assignment helps students learn to transfer learning from one context to another.

Sarah asks students to follow the model of the "whopper paragraph," one that includes a topic sentence, three supporting details, and a concluding sentence, and she models one of these paragraphs about a Harry Potter book. She also posts guidelines for whopper paragraphs on the SMART Board. Students write in their journals until the class is nearly over. There is just enough time for them to turn in their reading books and journals before it is time to move on to the next class.

## Transformational Learning: Sarah's Journey

Sarah was inspired to train as an elementary school teacher, but her first job was as a middle school science teacher, and she has chosen to remain at the middle school level ever since. "When I first began teaching English language arts, my curriculum was centered around a textbook," Sarah begins. "Over time, I began to focus on learning goals for my students instead of just moving through the textbook." Then she goes on to explain that as the standards movement evolved, so did the focus of her teaching. She has moved increasingly toward an emphasis on grade-level expectations that are derived from standards. "My team plans instruction around standards so we can incorporate novels and reading/writing workshop and still know we are hitting all the standards. We've been planning this way for three years; we're not having any difficulty transitioning to the CCSS," she explains.

The support of colleagues and administrators is important to Sarah's professional growth. She is enthusiastic about the workshop approach because "You're with the students, not sitting behind your desk," but she also recognizes that implementing it effectively takes time and effort. "Following a textbook from chapter to chapter was easier," she says, "but

**Honoring Diversity**

Giving students chances to engage in conversations about the texts they read enables them to connect their experiences to the experiences of characters in the novel; guiding these conversation opportunities can help students focus their ideas while also giving them a chance to voice their individual opinions.

**Connections**

The temptation to follow "canned curricula" or textbook schedules can be a tempting one in the age of standardization; however, Sarah learned that with the help of her colleagues, she could create a curriculum that more closely met the needs of her students. For more ideas about planning a curriculum that meets the needs of your students, see the resources in Section III.

I don't think my students learned as much." The transition to a workshop approach has been challenging, but she has learned a lot from the colleague with whom she alternates reading and writing workshops: "I had to have the support to really understand," she says. Her colleague, who also has an elementary school background, regularly invites other teachers to visit classes where she does writing workshop, and Sarah finds these opportunities for observation helpful. In addition, there is a workshop consultant who is available to teachers, and Sarah has learned a lot from her. "I dug my heels in at first," she says, "but these days I'm keeping a journal. It isn't easy. Now I know how my students feel."

The principal of Sarah's school offers support for teacher learning. "There is professional development at every staff meeting," Sarah explains. The principal also meets regularly with teacher leaders and department chairs to discuss curriculum and other issues surrounding student learning. "I personally feel included," Sarah claims. She is also confident that the transition to the CCSS will be easy because she and her colleagues are so accustomed to addressing state standards in their teaching. And she knows she can count on the support of a principal who sees a direct connection between the professional development of teachers and student achievement. She understands her principal's claim: "Professional development is not informational; it is transformational."

## Charting the Practices

The vignettes in this chapter illustrate how reading and writing workshops allow teachers the flexibility to adapt their instruction to their specific contexts and the needs of their students. Workshops also enable teachers to integrate multiple literacy activities—speaking, listening, writing, and reading. The following charts show how these teachers address specific standards in the CCSS in concert with NCTE principles to shape their teaching practices. The charts also include the learning practices students are expected to exhibit in response to the teaching practices.

## Common Core Standards That Intersect with These Practices

**Reading Standards for Literature, Grades 6–8**
5. Analyze how a particular sentence, chapter, scene, or stanza fits into the overall structure of a text and contributes to the development of the theme, setting, or plot.

| How Rick enacts the practice | ◄── Teaching Practice ──► | How Sarah enacts the practice |
|---|---|---|
| → Facilitates whole-class discussion about dialogue and models a text-based conversation.<br>→ Demonstrates how to create a wiki post and models how to write a response.<br>→ Uses formative assessment to check students' comprehension and fluency. | Teacher provides students with a variety of ways to engage with text through reading, writing, discussing, and use of technology. | → Teaches students terms and definitions for discussing characterization.<br>→ Directs students to find examples of different types of characters from class book.<br>→ Encourages students to question definitions to refine their understanding of character types. |
| **How Rick's students enact the practice** | ◄── **Learning Practice** ──► | **How Sarah's students enact the practice** |
| → Record examples of good dialogue on thinkmarks as they read.<br>→ Share their examples and explain their reasons to a partner; listen and respond to their partner's ideas.<br>→ Record their responses to text as wiki posts and respond thoughtfully to one another's posts. | Students interact with text in increasingly complex ways by reading, listening, speaking, writing, and using technology in whole-group and small-group settings. | → Discuss ideas and responses to text with classmates in a whole-class setting.<br>→ Listen and respond to classmates' ideas in pairs.<br>→ Apply their understanding of characterization to their independent reading.<br>→ Record examples and explanations in reading journals. |

### NCTE Principles
In reading instruction, emphasis should be placed on making meaning with text, including analysis of how text structures and features contribute to meaning.

*See pages 102–103 for more on NCTE principles regarding reading instruction.*

## Common Core Standards That Intersect with These Practices

**Speaking and Listening, Grades 6–8**

1. Engage effectively in a range of collaborative discussions (one-on-one, in groups, and teacher-led) with diverse partners on grade 6 topics, texts, and issues, building on others' ideas and expressing their own clearly.

| How Rick enacts the practice | ←—— Teaching Practice ——→ | How Sarah enacts the practice |
|---|---|---|
| → Organizes students into teams and pairs to discuss the day's class topic.<br>→ Conferences individually with students, asking them questions about the text.<br>→ Uses student volunteers to demonstrate examples to the class. | Teachers facilitate student learning through collaborative discussions, including pairs, teams, and teacher-led group exercises. | → Instructs the class as a whole and then asks students to talk with one another about the topic.<br>→ When students have difficulty in discussions, the teacher offers more information to help facilitate the discussion. |
| **How Rick's students enact the practice** | **←—— Learning Practice ——→** | **How Sarah's students enact the practice** |
| → Students discuss in pairs the topic of good dialogue.<br>→ Student pairs are willing to share their findings with the entire class.<br>→ Students volunteer to help the teacher make demonstrations to the class. | Students participate in collaborative discussions (pairs, teams, one-on-one) about the text, building on one another's knowledge and experiences. | → Students talk with one another, sometimes in pairs, about class topics and relevant real-life experiences that can be applied to class. |

### NCTE Principles

To ensure that all students have an opportunity to develop skills of informal speech, teachers should not depend exclusively on volunteers in class discussion.

Strategies for broadening participation include having all students respond in writing and then asking each student to respond aloud, asking students to discuss in pairs and report to the class, or distributing "talk tokens" that students can turn in after a contribution to a class discussion.

*See pages 106–107 for more on NCTE principles regarding speaking and listening.*

# Frames That Build: Exercises to Interpret the CCSS

The following are a few exercises for individuals or teams of teachers to use to work more with the standards and see how these vignettes may provide a lens through which to view your own interpretation and individualized implementation of the standards.

- *Reading the standards.* Read the writing standards for your grade level and look for any language about the use of technology in student writing. Consider how you already use writing technologies—from the pencil to online writing spaces—in your teaching. What new technologies could you include to help twenty-first-century learners in your classroom meet the demands of the CCSS?

- *Working across genres.* Students today need to be able to navigate multiple types of text, all of which have different demands on both their composers and their readers. Rick draws students' attention to specific language and punctuation features to help them understand dialogue, and he helps them understand the genre of the wiki by comparing it to conversation. Write down all of the genres with which you engage your students and consider your approach to those genres. How can you raise students' textual awareness as both readers and writers as you move across genres and engage students with many types of text?

# III

## Building

# ◎ Introduction

At this point, you may be thinking to yourself *Where do I begin?* There are many concerns competing for your attention as a teacher. Many students with diverse needs pass through your classroom door on a daily basis, and you have developed outcomes, goals, and objectives to guide your instruction in meeting these students' needs. To this end, you have established practices and ways of assessing student learning in your classroom. You bring your professional pedagogical content knowledge to the classroom, providing expertise in reading, writing, speaking, and listening for students. You teach within a specific context as well, considering the needs of your community and the demographic populations that you serve. With so many issues pressing in on teachers from all directions, aligning and shifting your teaching practices with the CCSS may feel like one more task heaped onto your already full plate.

Getting started by pulling back to view the big picture may help to put things into perspective and make first steps seem less overwhelming. As Figure 5.2 suggests, considering the CCSS as part of the deliberate teaching and learning choices you already make can continue to help you keep students at the center of instruction while planning, enacting teaching practices, and assessing student learning.

Just as most of us could not wake up one morning and decide to run a marathon on will alone without significant prior conditioning, so too it is important to remind yourself that planning, teaching, and assessing with the CCSS will not be instantaneous, but will become part of your ongoing work over time. In this section, we focus on building instruction *from* and *with* the CCSS. As noted in Section I, building with the CCSS in mind does not mean checking boxes for individual standards; it means integrating a careful examination of the CCSS with the contexts and practices of our classrooms, always putting students at the center. The chapters in this section offer three approaches to this process of building: individual, collaborator, and advocate.

- *Individual*—There *are* things that you individually can do to keep students at the center of your work. In this section we discuss how you can read the CCSS document to help you plan instruction with the CCSS.

- *Collaborator*—We invite you also to think about how to collaborate with colleagues in planning and assessing with the CCSS, especially within and across grade levels.

- *Advocate*—In this section, we explore how you can use your knowledge about the CCSS and their language, along with your collaborative efforts, to advocate for the professional supports that will help you advance your students' learning needs.

Rest assured that, as in marathon preparation, you cannot be expected to successfully tackle all three of these roles expertly as you begin your journey with the CCSS. Nor do we share these three roles to argue that you need to consider them sequentially or even fully. As you well know and as our experiences suggest, this process will be inherently like conditioning for a marathon. There will likely be great strides forward, plateaus, and at times struggles. But as the vignette teachers in this book illustrate, with the support of others near and far, holding the vision for what *can* be will sustain and affirm where you are headed.

# 5

# Individual Considerations:
# Keeping Students at the Center

I n reading this book, you have already begun considering how the CCSS pose new challenges that suggest you rethink and shift instruction. Reassure yourself that the CCSS do not have to call into question quality teaching practices, NCTE Principles, and research. But the CCSS may ask you to rethink the complexity of *what* you teach. The charts at the end of each vignette chapter are a beginning effort to illustrate *how* and *why* we can and should be concerned about helping students negotiate increasingly complex learning tasks and texts; additionally, this chapter will help further articulate *how* you can plan with this goal in mind.

## Reading the CCSS Document

The first step will be for you to individually negotiate and understand how the organization of the CCSS document requires close attention to detail. As we mentioned in Section I, the CCSS are grouped first by strands: K–5 and 6–12. These strands share strand sets, or College and Career Readiness Anchor Standards, in reading, writing, speaking and listening, and language. There are ten reading, ten writing, six speaking and listening, and six language Anchor Standards in each strand. Each Anchor Standard is then further detailed in grade-specific standards. The Anchor Standard is the foundation of the grade-specific standards, but the grade-specific standards include more specific language to further describe what the expectation is for students in each grade; therefore, there are some grade-specific standards that include sub-standards with numerals that further delineate such details. As Figure 5.1 illustrates, the grade-specific standards track for each grade level until ninth grade when the standards are grouped in two sets: ninth and tenth grades in the first set, and eleventh and twelfth grades in the second. The CCSS document describes this decision as one that was meant to reflect the numerous elective courses at the high school level where there are fewer grade-level-specific courses; at the middle school level, grades are still grouped individually. You will also

 **Collaboration**

At the 6–12 level, the Literacy in History/Social Studies, Science, and Technical Subjects strands share the reading and writing Anchor Standards. The CCSS send a strong message that reading and writing as part of developing student literacy within disciplinary specific classrooms is the responsibility of all teachers working together.

| | K–5 | 6–12 | |
|---|---|---|---|
| **Strands** | English Language Arts | English Language Arts | Literacy in History/Social Studies, Science, & Technical Subjects |

| Strand Sets — College & Career Readiness Anchor Standards |
|---|
| **Anchor Standard: Reading** |
| *Key Ideas and Details. Grades 6–12. Standard 2. Determine central ideas or themes of a text and analyze their development; summarize the key supporting details and ideas.* |

| **Grade-Specific Standards** | |
|---|---|
| **Reading, Standard 2.** | |
| **Grade** / **Literature** | **Informational Text** |

| Grade | Literature | Informational Text |
|---|---|---|
| 6 | Determine a theme or central idea of a text and how it is conveyed through particular details; provide a summary of the text distinct from personal opinions or judgments. | Determine a central idea of a text and how it is conveyed through particular details; provide a summary of the text distinct from personal opinions or judgment. |
| 7 | Determine a theme or central idea of a text and analyze its development over the course of the text; provide an objective summary of the text. | Determine two or more central ideas in a text and analyze their development over the course of the text; provide an objective summary of the text. |
| 8 | Determine a theme or central idea of a text and analyze its development over the course of the text, including its relationship to the characters, setting, and plot; provide an objective summary of the text. | Determine a central idea of a text and analyze its development over the course of the text, including its relationship to supporting ideas; provide an objective summary of the text. |

**FIGURE 5.1:** Reading the CCSS with an example.

notice that the CCSS focus a great deal on the kinds of reading students encounter across the school day, spelling out reading expectations for literature and informational texts. And at the K–5 level, the CCSS also include foundational skills standards.

An example of how this organization plays out in grades 6–8 may be helpful in explaining further. You'll note in Figure 5.1 an example of how you can read the CCSS for further specificity about grade-level distinctions using the first heading and Anchor Standard for reading.

When you read the CCSS document, we encourage you to read for these distinctions between grade-specific standards. This will help you identify *what* students in the grade(s) you teach will be expected to enact or demonstrate proficiency doing.

## Keeping Students at the Center

Reading the CCSS document with an eye toward distinguishing *what* students at the grade level(s) you teach will be expected to enact will help you keep your commitment to students at the center of your instructional decision making. Figure 5.2 illustrates how the multiple factors teachers consider when planning instruction speak

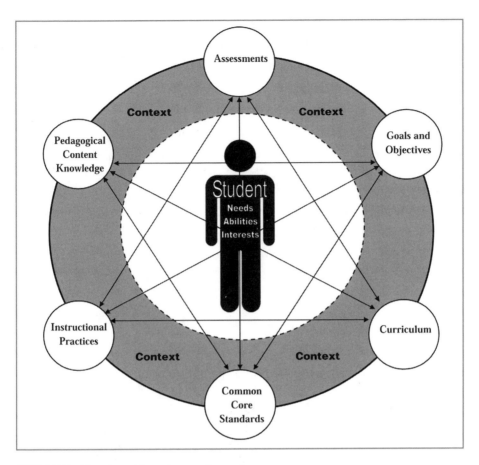

**FIGURE 5.2:** Planning with students at the center.

to one another through teachers' knowledge of and interaction with students. As a teacher, all of your work with students happens in close relation to the context where you teach, including your school and local community. So your students' needs, abilities, and interests—both individually and collectively—inform your decisions about planning for, enacting, and assessing instruction.

Keeping students at the center will enable you to prioritize what to attend to first and why. Furthermore, keeping students at the center may also empower you to utilize the CCSS mandate to advocate for your students' unique learning needs, as we discuss later in Chapter 7. Our collective teaching experiences across the country suggest challenges are inherent to good teaching, whether a result of the CCSS or not, but foregrounding student learning needs, abilities, and interests provides a useful and necessary lens through which to interpret and implement the CCSS. No matter the pathway you choose to begin, as Figure 5.2 illustrates, your students provide the map for planning and journeying with the CCSS.

Instruction that keeps students at the center often begins by asking what knowledge is available about the needs, abilities, and interests of student learners, and applying this knowledge to instructional decisions made about goals and objectives, curriculum, the CCSS, instructional practices, pedagogical content knowledge, and assessment. Figure 5.3 contains the types of questions you might ask yourself as you begin to consider the knowledge you have about students and how this can shape your instructional decisions in response to the CCSS. Answering the questions in Figure 5.3 also involves careful consideration of your teaching context in relation to what you know about your students by asking about the community, family and home cultures, out-of-school experiences, and school and district culture that influence your students' schooling experiences and your instructional decision making.

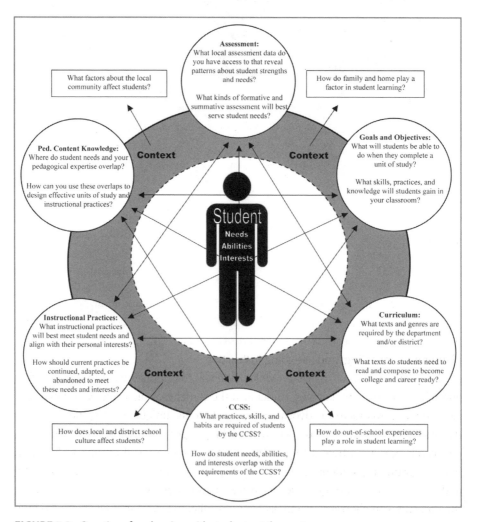

**FIGURE 5.3:** Questions for planning with students at the center.

Figure 5.4 provides a list of these questions that you can use as a beginning point for instructional planning. Your answers to these questions will help you enact teaching practices that support students' growing ability to make meaning of increasingly complex texts and enact increasingly complicated learning tasks. This approach, essential to the CCSS, can be described as spiraling instruction, and it's the approach that the vignette teachers you've read about use; below we detail how this approach can help guide your individual planning for the students in your classroom.

## Spiraling Instruction

As English language arts teachers, we know how difficult juggling the tasks of each day can be. Large class sizes, stacks of papers to grade, and limited collaborative and planning time often seem to get in the way of focusing fully on the needs of learners. At times, it may seem easier to plan lessons as lists of tasks just so you can make it smoothly through the day. In the past, we too have sometimes planned lessons in this way, using a monthly or a weekly calendar and filling the time with activities that aim in an unarticulated way at the objectives, skills, and practices we have in mind for students. Over time, however, we have come to view our planning differently, and this shift in our thinking and planning has actually increased the quality and complexity of the thinking and work of our students. In large part, this shift in our practice resulted from understanding how ELA instruction may differ from other content areas.

Unlike other content area instruction, which might be seen as building students' understandings and skills linearly, ELA learning can be seen as spiraling recursively. Research supports instructional planning that provides students with multiple opportunities to revisit concepts and enact their learning over time with increasing difficulty as more successful than planning and instruction that marches students through sets of activities and tasks. Planning this kind of instruction that spirals learning affords students opportunities to develop ELA understandings and skills within and across lessons, units of study, and courses.

As we've already discussed and as Figures 1.1 and 5.1 help to illustrate, the CCSS embed text complexity within the Anchor Standards. Thus, increasing the complexity of tasks and reading is one way to spiral your instruction. Additionally, the grade-level-specific standards grouped around the same Anchor Standards can prove helpful in that they point out specific skills and practices students can work on in a particular grade level and suggest the expectation that students will add to and refine these skills as they move from one grade to the next. Spiraling instruction within grade levels is often referred to as horizontal alignment whereas spiraling instruction across grade levels is often referred to as vertical alignment. The organization of the CCSS, as outlined in Figure 1.1, can help you consider how to plan and align

What do I know about my **students** that supports my planning?

- Their needs –


- Their abilities –


- Their interests –


- Including:
    o  Their home and heritage languages –


    o  The funds of knowledge they bring from their homes and local communities –


    o  The literacies students bring into the classroom –


### Your Local Context

What factors about the local community affect students?


How do family and home play a factor in student learning?


How do out-of-school experiences play a role in student learning?


How does local and district school culture affect students?


**FIGURE 5.4:** Questions for planning template.

| Assessment | Goals and Objectives |
|---|---|
| What local assessment data do you have access to that reveal patterns about student strengths and needs? | What will students be able to do when they complete a unit of study? |
| What kinds of formative and summative assessment will best serve student needs? | What skills, practices, and knowledge will students gain in your classroom? |

| Curriculum | CCSS |
|---|---|
| What texts and genres are required by the department and/or school district? | What practices, skills, and habits are required of students by the CCSS? |
| What texts do students need to read and compose to become college and career ready? | How do student needs, abilities, and interests overlap with the requirements of the CCSS? |

| Instructional Practices | Pedagogical Content Knowledge |
|---|---|
| What instructional practices will best meet student needs and align with their personal interests? | Where do student needs and your pedagogical expertise overlap? |
| How should current practices be continued, adapted, or abandoned to meet these needs and interests? | How can you use these overlaps to design effective units of study and instructional practices? |

(Figure 5.4 continued)

ELA instruction horizontally and vertically. Below, we'll focus on how you can plan instruction that spirals in your own classroom, but in Chapter 6, we'll return to this idea of horizontal and vertical alignment through a discussion of collaboration.

## Planning Units of Study

**Connections**

"Units of study," in the chapters that follow, refers not to the teaching of specific texts but to designing groups of tasks, activities, and assessments that seek to meet an articulated set of goals, objectives, essential questions, themes, or genres.

Identifying how to begin planning units of study that spiral ELA instruction and meet the CCSS demands can feel like a daunting task. But after identifying CCSS grade-specific expectations as well as your local approaches to asking students to demonstrate the learning and skills these expectations outline, you'll be ready to consider planning units.

Whether you are designing for the first time or revisiting previously taught units of study with your students' needs as the primary lens for shaping your instruction, there are multiple ways that you might choose to develop your units of study. The following list highlights some of the overarching approaches other ELA teachers have chosen to guide the development of their units of study:

- *Thematic*—around themes that ask students to grapple with shared human experiences (e.g., loss, love, courage, heroism, empathy)

- *Essential questions*—around questions worthy of students' attention without easy right or wrong answers that ask students to seek understanding to act with resolve; many of these questions illuminate what it means to be human, how humans choose to respond to pressing issues, and ask students to wrestle with uncertainty and complexity (e.g., Under what circumstances are people justified in questioning authority? What is the cost of progress? Why is literature worthy of study?)

- *Genre study*—around particular genres or multigenres that offer students opportunities to study literature within the genre as fulcrum texts for students' writing in and speaking about the genre (e.g., narrative, short story, poetry, drama, essay, website)

None of these approaches is inherently better than the others. Rather, we suggest that whichever approach you choose, you can begin with student learning needs to spiral instruction and therefore learning toward further complexity. For example, if you wanted to organize your units thematically, you might begin using answers to Figure 5.4 questions to identify a theme that you know your students will find engaging and relevant as they read and write texts around the theme throughout the unit.

Reading Anchor Standard 9 deals specifically with thematic understanding, so you can ask students to wrestle with theme in each unit (in addition to targeting other standards) by building on the expectations from a previous unit. Through this process, students will have to apply prior learning to a new theme and texts with new, more complex skills, strategies, and thinking.

## Choosing Resources

With an organizational scheme in mind, in the early stages of unit planning, teachers often consider the texts they will use in a unit. We recognize that many districts or schools have adopted core texts or fulcrum texts that serve as the foundation of particular units of study. Identifying these and other resources in support of a unit's focus that meets the CCSS demands is an important consideration. As our earlier discussions in Section I affirmed, it will be important to also consider when choosing resources that the CCSS do encourage the unification of ELA strand sets (reading, writing, speaking and listening, and language) so that each unit of study integrates standards from each strand set (see Figure 1.1).

**Connections**

A useful and current definition of *text* clearly includes print materials such as books, novels, short stories, and poetry, but also expands to include other types of twenty-first-century documents such as newspaper and magazine articles, webpages, film and video, and even audio and sound clips. Expanding our notions of what counts as a text in classrooms is part of encouraging our students to develop multiple literacies.

We agree that teachers and students need greater access to a wider range of texts. Hopefully, the CCSS will raise awareness of why students would benefit from access to such materials, especially since the CCSS do raise awareness of the value of students' use of increasingly complex texts—both literature and informational. But we also acknowledge, based on our own experience, the range of choice that exists in different schools. For some of us, choice means selecting what was already available and finding free or reproducible alternatives when possible. For others, choice means the opportunity to order resources in support of unit objectives. There are unique challenges that each context poses. For those with little choice, considering how to help students meet the CCSS demands can seem nearly impossible.

Nonetheless, you can use a small sampling of various texts, even in different genres and modes, to help students navigate complex texts. In Rod's class, for example, he uses literature to discuss the differences youth can make in society, communities, and families. In addition, though, he chooses articles from magazines and Internet sites to support the main text. As we learn more about text complexity and the ways to help our students navigate these texts, we recognize that we will all need to at least begin with what we have in our resource shelves and rooms. But the issue of pressing import may be less about what materials we have than what we do or, better yet, what we ask students to do. We can best focus our energies on going more deeply with fewer texts of greater complexity than on breadth and coverage. Resource choices should be made in conjunction with choices about unit objectives and goals that will help students meet the CCSS and more.

## Beginning with the End in Mind: Scaffolding Assessment throughout a Unit of Study

Because the CCSS are a set of grade-level expectations, they focus on outcomes. That is to say, the CCSS articulate what students should be able to do at the end of a particular grade. The CCSS, as well as good unit design and planning, suggest that we begin planning with the end in mind—that we keep omnipresent in our minds and on paper the ultimate goal we have for students. Figure 5.5, the unit plan template, provides one frame for thinking through and logging your plans for a unit of study.

We suggest that once you've identified the focus for a particular unit of study, you begin by identifying the outcome of the unit or what students will be expected

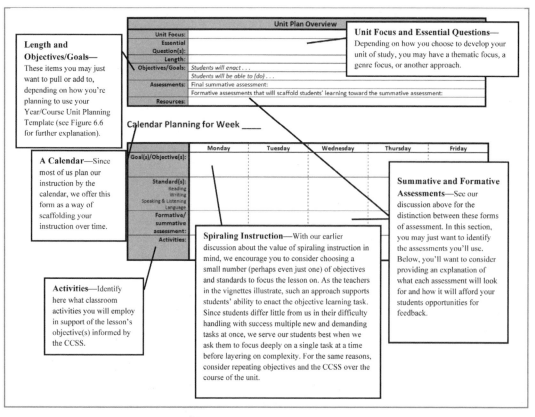

**FIGURE 5.5:** Unit plan template.

to do at the end of the unit. Your unit objectives and goals will help you articulate what learning or tasks students will be able to enact at the end of the unit. Put another way, you'll want to identify the summative assessment that you'll ask students to complete at the end of the unit. Summative assessments focus on reporting whether students have met proficiency in demonstrating their ability to enact unit objectives. Often, summative assessments take the form of essays or presentations, but as NCTE notes at www.ncte.org/books/supp-students-6-8, there are many other forms of summative assessment.

Web 5.1

Although the CCSS are finally about what happens in the end, it is also important to note that the CCSS are not exhaustive. The CCSS need not limit the scope of your instruction. Yes, they set the minimum, but you can define the upper limits of your instruction and expectations for students as you plan instruction.

Similarly, it is critical to keep in mind that teacher-developed formative assessments will ultimately have the greatest influence on shaping the instruction and learning experiences that support students' ability to perform well on summative assessments. Multiple formative assessments strategically employed throughout a unit support ongoing learning and instruction. We see this in Rick's class as he works with students regularly using the workshop approach to teaching. In this setting, he conferences with students, which helps him identify if students are understanding and mastering the material in reading and writing. As the NCTE Research Policy Brief "Fostering High-Quality Formative Assessment" details, high-quality formative assessments offer students *and* teachers more immediate feedback on students' ability to enact a specific learning task. This feedback helps students know how and why they can proceed in working to enact the task or in progressing toward the next task (part of spiraling instruction and learning). For teachers, formative assessments inform instructional decision making and interventions in helping to ensure that all students are able to meet proficiency on the summative assessment task(s).

Given the instructional and learning value of formative assessments, you will want to identify the formative assessments you'll include in your unit of study. The formative assessments you identify and design should help both you and your students identify where, when, and how to intervene in support of their learning and ability to enact the objectives, or learning tasks, throughout the unit. The formative assessments you choose should therefore come at critical points in the unit when you will be asking students to try out or enact new and difficult tasks. As you may already know or infer from the discussion thus far, formative assessments are not focused on grading students. Rather, formative assessments are focused on providing you and your students with feedback that will guide subsequent teaching and learning. This feedback will influence their later performance on the summative assessment. Collectively, the formative assessments you scaffold throughout the unit should help build students' ability and confidence in demonstrating proficiency on the later summative assessment(s).

Figure 5.5 offers further details about the type of planning thoughts you might want to record as you build or revise a unit of study with the end in mind.

## Planning and Organizing Units across the Year or Semester

Identifying individual units of study cannot occur without simultaneously considering how multiple units of study progress across the year or semester (depending on the grade level). When Mary plans her year, she looks for an applicable theme to weave into her lessons. She chooses fulcrum texts that can help her achieve her goal, those that connect young people to positive change in the world (social responsibility) and that encourage them to extend themselves through expository/argumentative writing and self-expression.

As we have discussed, these considerations are a part of the spiraling that you can plan for across units of study. For example, teachers who choose a genre approach might begin with a personal narrative unit of study where students review prior learning from a previous course or grade level about reading thinking strategies and writing strategies for developing ideas. In a later short-story unit, teachers might spiral students' learning by revisiting reading and thinking strategies in this new genre to explore with students how readers approach different kinds of texts. At the same time, teachers could introduce greater complexity in one or more of the thinking strategies they ask students to enact. And in terms of writing instruction, teachers might spiral instruction by building on earlier ways they invited students to develop ideas within a paragraph to consider how idea development works across paragraphs complicated by learning how this works in a new genre.

As you develop individual units of study in relation to other units, Figure 5.6 can serve as a tool for logging how you plan to spiral instruction within and across units of study. The pull-out boxes below offer further details about the type of planning thoughts you might want to record in each box.

Just as instruction spirals across a unit of study, so too does formative assessment. As students encounter new and increasingly difficult tasks, immediate feedback via formative assessments helps to build students' confidence and commitment to the task at hand. This is because the formative assessment helps students identify which areas they need to focus on and teachers can clarify misunderstanding. Formative assessments therefore boost students' learning across a unit of study; these formative assessments support students' improvement over time and ability to negotiate increasingly demanding tasks with independence.

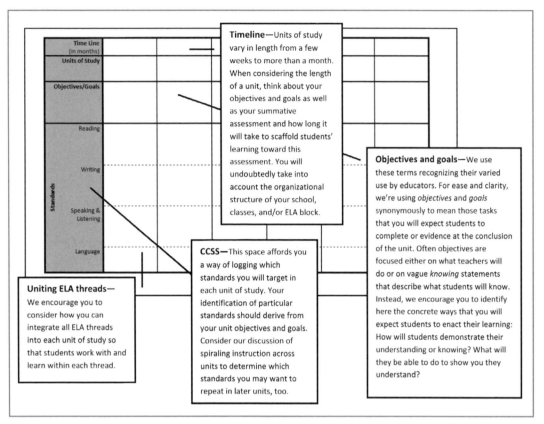

Standards

| Time Line (in months) | Units of Study | Objectives/Goals | Reading | Writing | Speaking & Listening | Language |

**Timeline**—Units of study vary in length from a few weeks to more than a month. When considering the length of a unit, think about your objectives and goals as well as your summative assessment and how long it will take to scaffold students' learning toward this assessment. You will undoubtedly take into account the organizational structure of your school, classes, and/or ELA block.

**Objectives and goals**—We use these terms recognizing their varied use by educators. For ease and clarity, we're using *objectives* and *goals* synonymously to mean those tasks that you will expect students to complete or evidence at the conclusion of the unit. Often objectives are focused either on what teachers will do or on vague *knowing* statements that describe what students will know. Instead, we encourage you to identify here the concrete ways that you will expect students to enact their learning: How will students demonstrate their understanding or knowing? What will they be able to do to show you they understand?

**CCSS**—This space affords you a way of logging which standards you will target in each unit of study. Your identification of particular standards should derive from your unit objectives and goals. Consider our discussion of spiraling instruction across units to determine which standards you may want to repeat in later units, too.

**Uniting ELA threads**—We encourage you to consider how you can integrate all ELA threads into each unit of study so that students work with and learn within each thread.

**FIGURE 5.6:** Year/course unit planning template.

The chapters included in Section II provide a useful tool for thinking as you consider planning your own units of study. We do not offer them as packages to adopt; after all, such an approach might not take into consideration the unique contextual factors influencing your decision making, including, most notably, what you know about your students.

# 6

# Working Collaboratively to Enact the CCSS

As we have mentioned throughout the book, planning and teaching are collaborative processes strengthened with the support of colleagues. In Chapter 5, we discussed how your ongoing journey with the CCSS will centrally involve the students in your classroom, but your ability to positively affect student learning is largely influenced by the relationships you foster with colleagues as well. In this chapter, we suggest ways that teachers can work collaboratively to support one another and thereby their students.

## Collaborate on Literacy across the Curriculum

The teachers' voices represented in this book and our ongoing conversations with colleagues across the nation reveal just how imperative collaborative efforts to understand and enact the CCSS are to the sustainability of our joint efforts. Many teachers—and administrators—are surprised to learn that the CCSS themselves urge us toward such aims. As we discussed earlier in our overview of the CCSS document and in Section I, the CCSS argue on page 7 that students who are college and career ready ought to be able to respond to a range of disciplinary demands, tasks, audiences, and purposes for writing, reading, speaking, and listening. The CCSS's inclusion of College and Career Readiness Anchor Standards at the 6–12 grade levels for literacy in history/social science, science, and technical subjects sends a strong message that *with* our colleagues in these other content areas we are jointly responsible for helping students navigate the range of these literacy demands. Therefore, the CCSS recognize what we ELA teachers have long understood: we alone cannot take on the burden of equipping students to become literate consumers and producers of *all* content area knowledge. When some teachers read on page 5 of the CCSS document that by eighth grade, 45 percent of the sum of students' reading should be literary and the other 55 percent informational, they assume that this means that

**Web 6.1**

Go online for other resources for building schoolwide literacy initiatives.

they will need to devote 55 percent of students' ELA course reading to informational texts. However, consistent with this literacy across the content areas focus, the CCSS footnote to the chart with these percentages indicates that these targets are representative of students' reading of diverse texts across courses throughout their school day. Similarly, the CCSS spell out that the sum of eighth-grade students' writing should include students' writing in ELA *and* non-ELA settings so that 35 percent of students' writing across courses will be to persuade, 35 percent to explain, and 30 percent to convey experience. It is therefore important for us to work with colleagues across content areas to determine how best to jointly support students' reading and writing across the school day in the range of their coursework.

## Look for Opportunities to Form Professional Learning Groups and Communities

Professional learning groups and communities are powerful locations for teacher growth, development, and collaboration. As you work collaboratively with your colleagues, grade-level band, and department, look for opportunities to initiate authentic, inquiry-driven professional learning communities. A professional learning group can be a place to house discussion about the CCSS, NCTE principles, NCTE policy briefs, NCTE Web seminars, or professional books. To help you begin imagining new ways to engage in collaboration at your school, we have provided a few possible suggestions. These various opportunities for collaboration can strengthen communities of learning as they address the CCSS.

- *Start a Teachers as Readers Book Group.* Some professional learning communities are designed as book clubs. Members read and discuss children's and young adults' literature along with professional texts.

- *Take advantage of collaborative spaces.* Departmental meetings can be great places to work collaboratively with colleagues. In some schools, this will mean rethinking current views about departmental meetings. Often, with the best intentions, these spaces focus primarily on logistical issues with little support for teachers to draw on their own backgrounds and styles and embrace the strengths and needs of their students, but departmental meetings can be spaces where professional planning is grounded in a commitment to the autonomy of knowledgeable teachers who make decisions for and with their students. With such a view, departmental meetings can be places where teachers engage in professional study and reflection that supports growth in the company of colleagues who are wrestling with similar issues.

- *Attend national conferences.* Attending professional conferences is a fabulous way for teachers to find space and support for focused reflection. Through these experiences, teachers share their great work and learn from others in ways that will ultimately enhance successful teaching in their home districts and schools. Conferences support teachers by giving them opportunities to become intellectually reinvigorated by engaging with colleagues from across the country.

- *Seek out online forums.* Online forums are another space for reflection and growth. Participating in such forums, teachers gain insights from across the country as they have opportunities to share their work and learn from others' classrooms. With other teachers, they address challenges, pose questions, provide insight, and find new ideas about practice, materials, and other resources.

**Web 6.3**

## Plan, Develop, and Assess with the CCSS

**Connections**

As these teachers' practices illustrate, the CCSS need not overshadow the particularities of the places in which we all teach.

The CCSS document details grade-specific expectations, but questions about how students will be asked to demonstrate the standard-specific task of understanding are left to teachers' collective expertise. To be clear, the CCSS do not advocate for particular ELA pedagogy. Therefore, collaborating with colleagues in your school, district, region, and state can help you localize the CCSS; together you can interpret the CCSS language and plan to enact the CCSS grade-level expectations in the ways most responsive to your local context.

### Identify Grade-Level Distinctions

Figure 6.1 builds on our conversations about how to read the CCSS document for grade-level differences. This model can help you and your colleagues extend your initial individual thinking about horizontal and vertical alignment in relation to the CCSS document. The figure serves as a tool for articulating how you will ask students to demonstrate grade-level distinctions and what they will look like in your classrooms. By noting in the boxes what language is added or changed in the progression from grade to grade and how this language might translate to instructional choices and student activities, Figure 6.1 can be used on three levels:

- Level 1: to identify CCSS Anchor Standards distinctions across grade levels
- Level 2: to identify the learning tasks that students will need to enact to demonstrate proficiency in meeting each standard

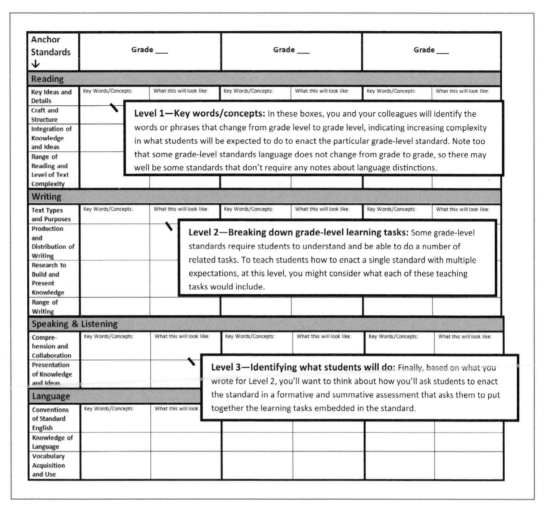

| Anchor Standards ↓ | Grade ___ | | Grade ___ | | Grade ___ | |
|---|---|---|---|---|---|---|
| **Reading** | | | | | | |
| Key Ideas and Details | Key Words/Concepts: | What this will look like: | Key Words/Concepts: | What this will look like: | Key Words/Concepts: | What this will look like: |
| Craft and Structure | | | | | | |
| Integration of Knowledge and Ideas | | | | | | |
| Range of Reading and Level of Text Complexity | | | | | | |
| **Writing** | | | | | | |
| Text Types and Purposes | Key Words/Concepts: | What this will look like: | Key Words/Concepts: | What this will look like: | Key Words/Concepts: | What this will look like: |
| Production and Distribution of Writing | | | | | | |
| Research to Build and Present Knowledge | | | | | | |
| Range of Writing | | | | | | |
| **Speaking & Listening** | | | | | | |
| Comprehension and Collaboration | Key Words/Concepts: | What this will look like: | Key Words/Concepts: | What this will look like: | Key Words/Concepts: | What this will look like: |
| Presentation of Knowledge and Ideas | | | | | | |
| **Language** | | | | | | |
| Conventions of Standard English | Key Words/Concepts: | What this will look | | | | |
| Knowledge of Language | | | | | | |
| Vocabulary Acquisition and Use | | | | | | |

**Level 1—Key words/concepts:** In these boxes, you and your colleagues will identify the words or phrases that change from grade level to grade level, indicating increasing complexity in what students will be expected to do to enact the particular grade-level standard. Note too that some grade-level standards language does not change from grade to grade, so there may well be some standards that don't require any notes about language distinctions.

**Level 2—Breaking down grade-level learning tasks:** Some grade-level standards require students to understand and be able to do a number of related tasks. To teach students how to enact a single standard with multiple expectations, at this level, you might consider what each of these teaching tasks would include.

**Level 3—Identifying what students will do:** Finally, based on what you wrote for Level 2, you'll want to think about how you'll ask students to enact the standard in a formative and summative assessment that asks them to put together the learning tasks embedded in the standard.

**FIGURE 6.1:** Grade-level distinctions planning template.

- Level 3: to identify what you'll ask your students to do to enact the CCSS articulated expectations; in this level, together you can identify common formative and summative assessments you might use within and/or across grade levels

You can therefore use this document three separate times or for three separate passes to examine and discuss each focus level. Or you could choose to focus on a single level that offers you a way to scaffold conversations with your colleagues. The textboxes help to explain how Figure 6.1 can be used at each level.

In Figure 6.2, we provide an example of how you might use this document at all three levels using Anchor Speaking and Listening Standard 4. The pull-outs highlight further the thinking at each level of discussion.

It is important to note that this chart does not need to replace your existing tools and resources for mapping curriculum. Instead, it offers one way to help you think through the grade-level distinctions in conversations with others.

## Plan Common Course or Grade-Level Instruction

Understanding the grade-level distinctions using Figure 6.1 might also encourage you to consider ways to plan instruction with others who teach the same course or grade-level. You can focus together on integrating ELA threads as well. We encourage you to consider using Figures 5.5 and 5.6 to facilitate your discussions and plans with colleagues who teach the same grade level or course as well as department colleagues who can help you think about spiraling instruction from previous grades and courses for students.

## Identify Common Texts

Meeting in grade level, course teams, or departments to develop units around core, or fulcrum, texts can be a useful way to align instruction with the CCSS. Using common texts can be a way to reorient your conversations toward students' ability to enact learning tasks, and you can share common experiences to adapt instruction while still feeling at liberty to pick context and texture texts. Together you can ask questions as you begin planning about which texts to choose and why:

- What young adult novels, poems, nonfiction articles, or other texts could supplement fulcrum texts?
- How can we incorporate other ELA threads in our discussion of and writing about chosen texts?
- How can we integrate digital technology or multimodal opportunities for students to enact CCSS learning tasks as they read and compose texts?
- How can we support struggling or reluctant readers with the chosen fulcrum texts?

## Select and Enact a New Teaching Strategy

Beyond planning together, trying out a new teaching strategy in your classroom can be easier when you do it with one or two other teachers. The CCSS invite teachers to

| Anchor Standards | Grade 6 | | Grade 7 | |
|---|---|---|---|---|
| **Speaking** | | | | |
| Presentation of Knowledge and Ideas #4 | Key Words/ Concepts:<br><br>1st Level—Present claims and findings, sequencing ideas logically and using pertinent descriptions, facts, and details to accentuate main ideas or themes; use appropriate eye contact, adequate volume, and clear pronounciation. | What this will look like:<br><br>2nd Level—<br>• Present claims, findings logically<br>• Emphasize main ideas by foregrounding them in the introduction and conclusion<br>• Deliver ideas clearly so that the audience can hear and understand<br><br>3rd Level—In units 1–3 in response to the core text:<br><br>• Present an opinion about a character to the class, connecting it to a theme from the text and using descriptions of the character | Key Words/ Concepts:<br><br>1st Level—<br>*In addition to 6:*<br>• Emphasize salient points<br>• Give examples<br>• Provide information in a coherently organized way | What this will look like:<br><br>2nd Level—<br>*In addition to 6:*<br>• Make main idea clear to the audience<br>• Give specific examples to support claims and opinions<br>• llustrate the ability to structure a speech in a logical way, using transitions<br><br>3rd Level—In units 1–3 in response to the core text:<br><br>• Layer in examples from the text, quotes from the text<br>• Focus on theme, connection to main idea of the text |

Level 1—Here it may be easier to begin with the first grade level by writing the full standard or by listing key words. Because of the density of this standard, we chose to list the entire standard.

Level 1—In each subsequent grade level, you might just add what other items are mentioned or in some other way indicate differences from the earlier grade(s).

Level 2—We thought about each of the different learning tasks that students would need to enact to demonstrate successful proficiency in meeting this standard.

Level 3—You'll notice that we have just begun this level. We are noting what units might take into account which learning tasks. Remember that not every unit need expect students to enact all of the learning tasks for each standard. This is part of the power of spiraled instruction, where you can return to standards with increasing complexity over the course of the semester, year, or course.

**FIGURE 6.2:** Grade-level distinctions example.

study how particular instructional practices support student learning and the ability to demonstrate proficiency in meeting and exceeding the CCSS expectations. If your building has a literacy specialist or lead literacy teacher, you can ask him or her to help you plan and give you feedback or you can build a study group focused on action research with other colleagues. Once you try out the new strategy, evaluate the results using joint learning goals and objectives, and work together to tweak and repeat. Your group can also share your results with your grade-level group or department.

### Develop Common Assessments

The example in Figure 6.2 invites you to consider how you might collaboratively identify, develop, and adapt common formative and summative assessments within grade levels or courses taught by more than one teacher. Some teacher learning communities use common assessments to review their instruction as well as students' work throughout units of study. Because they share the assessments and the language, making adjustments to instruction in the midst of units and in relation to future units becomes a shared responsibility. In this way, these teachers remain ever responsive to their students' learning needs and ultimately to their students' ability to enact unit learning tasks that demonstrate their ability to meet the CCSS demands.

### Share Ideas Online with Colleagues Near and Far

We encourage you to share your efforts and ideas in online professional forums and with your colleagues in your professional learning communities. Because all

**Web 6.4**

of the figures and charts throughout this book are also available for your use and adaptation on www.ncte.org/books/supp-students-6-8, we hope you will share your thinking related to, experiences using, and revision of these resources and your thoughts about the CCSS more generally there. Supporting one another online in such a forum is one way to strengthen our ability to help students meet the CCSS demands and to remind ourselves that colleagues nationwide are negotiating similar challenges. You can also find interactive lesson plans at www.readwritethink.org, or contribute some of your own.

In a profession where we all largely perform the obligations and duties of our role as ELA teachers alone in our classrooms, it is critically important to remember that you are not alone in this effort to enact the CCSS. We hope the teachers you've met in Section II highlight the powerful potential of uniting with others who share the challenge of meeting the CCSS demands.

# 7

# Becoming a Teacher Advocate

The teachers featured in Section II highlight powerful ways of leveraging the CCSS to shape instruction that meets students' needs and prepares them to contribute to a world we can only imagine today. These teachers, however, are but a few of the thousands of committed ELA K–12 teachers who share this goal, including you. Part of your strength and expertise as an ELA teacher and/or instructional leader is your ability to advocate for your own professional needs and therefore your students' learning needs in collaboration with others near and far. Your commitment to reading this book, to learning about how the CCSS intersect with your teaching practices, and to working with others to learn and plan together illustrates your concern for keeping students at the center.

Throughout this book we have discussed ways in which you can work individually and collaboratively to make sense of, put into perspective, and act in relation to the CCSS; in this brief final section, we invite you to begin considering how you can work to advocate locally, within your state, and even nationally in equally important small and large ways for the support that will enable you to sustain professional learning and practices in support of students' needs. Below we highlight by building on earlier conversations ways that you can begin this advocacy work.

## Advocate for Yourself by Committing to Continued Professional Growth

Every teacher knows that professional autonomy is not a given. When discussing standards or other guidelines, it is important to be alert to tendencies to look at the CCSS as a means to homogenize ways of teaching and students' pathways to learning. At the same time, teachers have a responsibility to meet their side of the bargain. As teachers, we cannot claim the right to autonomy without committing to ongoing, focused professional growth.

## Advocate for Your Students by Using Knowledge of Your Context to Design Instruction

Rigid interpretations of standards often lead to the imposition of rigid pacing guides and scripted programs that tell teachers what to do and say. Scripted programs limit what teachers can do in their classrooms by failing to draw on their professional knowledge. Work together in schools and districts to ensure that standards are used knowledgeably and responsibly so that policies never deny teachers their ability to use their professional knowledge.

## Advocate for Instruction That Is Student Centered

We know that using the cultural heritages, orientations, and resources of ethnically and racially diverse students helps them learn. Seek, find, celebrate, and utilize the rich languages and literacies that exist in the homes and communities of your students. Students also bring diverse learning styles and enormous variations and abilities; consider these in developing instruction. Fill your classrooms and the halls of your schools with wide varieties of languages, literacies, and abilities. Teach about them and teach through them. Because our choice in resources ought to be guided by the overarching goals and purposes that guide our planning units of study, we can best persuade internal and external stakeholders about the worth and necessity of such resources when we can also provide a compelling rationale. The best rationale centers on student achievement.

## Advocate for the Use of Locally Developed Formative Assessments

It is critically important to recognize your professional expertise in developing formative assessments that speak with specificity to your students' learning needs. You know the local needs of your students and the community that supports their learning in and out of school. Therefore, you and your colleagues are best suited to design, implement, and adjust the formative assessments that will best enable your students to meet the demands of the CCSS. Speaking with colleagues both near and far will enable you to speak compellingly with local and national stakeholders about how your locally designed, implemented, and adjusted formative assessments best meet your students' needs and are still responsive to the CCSS.

## Advocate for Your Students by Contributing to Larger Professional Communities

When our days are consumed by the immediate needs of our students and colleagues, it can feel overwhelming to think of joining other colleagues from afar. Alternately, you may wonder what you have to contribute to a larger professional community beyond your school or district. But you can rest assured that the time and energy necessary to do so are well worth it and less extensive than you might think. You do have a lot to share with others; your experiences are worthy of others' attention. And professional organizations such as NCTE are a renewing space to remind yourself of this and to find solace and empowerment, especially as you meet the challenges of the CCSS.

We share your concern about the onslaught of attacks against teachers, including ELA teachers, by those who question our professional knowledge. Connecting with others near and far to give voice to your expertise is one amazingly powerful way to begin speaking back persuasively. And in this time of the CCSS, we believe in the work illustrated by the teachers featured in Section II and similarly enacted by teachers like you across this country. Your teaching practices and efforts to keep students at the center illustrate that the CCSS can be leveraged toward powerful ends by those of us who do the work that matters daily with the students in our lives. By connecting with one another locally, regionally, and nationally, we have the power to influence what the CCSS will become by joining the conversation. But it's more than just connecting. By equipping ourselves with the knowledge that comes from observing the CCSS deeply and from centering our CCSS-informed instruction on our knowledge of local contexts, we can join with teachers locally, nationally, and internationally in building instructional practices that will enable students to develop the habits that lead to becoming flexible, adaptive readers, writers, thinkers, and doers who are ready to meet the challenges of the twenty-first century.

# Appendix A

## *Resources*

Following is a consolidation of professional resources provided throughout and in support of the issues and concepts discussed in this text. These resources could serve educators' ongoing discussions, study groups, and individual inquiries equally well.

| Topic | Resource |
|---|---|
| Instruction for struggling readers | Allington, Richard L. "Intervention All Day Long: New Hope for Struggling Readers." *Voices from the Middle* 14.4 (2007): 7–14. Print. |
| | Calhoon, Mary Beth, Alexia Sandow, and Charles V. Hunter. "Reorganizing the Instructional Reading Components: Could There Be a Better Way to Design Remedial Reading Programs to Maximize Middle School Students with Reading Disabilities' Response to Treatment?" *Annals of Dyslexia* 60.1 (2010): 57–85. Print. |
| | Kelley, Joan G., Nonie K. Lesaux, Michael J. Kieffer, and S. Elisabeth Faller. "Effective Academic Vocabulary Instruction in the Urban Middle School. *The Reading Teacher* 64.1 (2010): 5–14. Print. |
| Literacy practices | Alvermann, Donna E. "Literacy on the Edge: How Close Are We to Closing the Literacy Achievement Gap?" *Voices from the Middle* 13.1 (2005): 8–14. Print. |
| | Alvermann, Donna E. "Youth in the Middle: Our Guides to Improved Literacy Instruction?" *Voices from the Middle* 14.2 (2006): 7–13. Print. |
| | Beers, Kylene, Robert E. Probst, and Linda Rief, eds. *Adolescent Literacy: Turning Promise into Practice.* Portsmouth, NH: Heinemann, 2007. Print. |
| | Bomer, Randy. *Building Adolescent Literacy in Today's English Classrooms.* Portsmouth, NH: Heinemann, 2011. Print. |
| | Fisher, Douglas, and Nancy Frey. "What Does It Take to Create Skilled Readers? Facilitating the Transfer and Application of Literacy Strategies." *Voices from the Middle* 15.4 (2008): 16–22. Print. |
| | Hirai, Debra L. Cook, Irene Borrego, Emilio Garza, and Carl T. Kloock, with Deborrah Wakelee and Vicki Murray. *Academic Language/Literacy Strategies for Adolescents: A "How To" Manual for Educators.* New York: Routledge, 2010. Print. |
| | Jetton, Tamara L., and Janice A. Dole, eds. *Adolescent Literacy Research and Practice.* New York: Guilford, 2004. Print. |

| Topic | Resource |
|---|---|
| Literacy practices *(continued)* | McCord, Noah. "A Student Perspective and Observations of Engaging Literacy Experiences." *Voices from the Middle* 18.3 (2011): 38–41. Print. |
| | National Council of Teachers of English. *Adolescent Literacy: An NCTE Policy Research Brief.* Web. Retrieved from http://www.ncte.org/library/NCTEFiles/Resources/PolicyResearch/AdolLitResearchBrief.pdf |
| | Radcliffe, Barbara. "'Stuck in the Middle': Helping Students Begin New Literacy Lives." *Voices from the Middle* 15.2 (2007): 18–29. Print. |
| | Wilhelm, Jeffrey D., and Bruce Novak. *Teaching Literacy for Love and Wisdom: Being the Book and Being the Change.* New York: Teachers College Press; Urbana, IL: NCTE; Berkeley, CA: NWP, 2011. Print. |
| Peer communities/ classroom communities | Anderson, Jeff. "The Express-Lane Edit: Making Editing Useful for Young Adolescents." *Voices from the Middle* 15.4 (2008): 40–44. Print. |
| | Bryant, Jill, and Stephen Daniels. "Power, Voice, and Empowerment: Classroom Committees in a Middle Level Language Arts Curriculum." *Voices from the Middle* 16.1 (2008): 31–41. Print. |
| | Hansen, Jane. "'The Way They Act Around a Bunch of People': Seventh-Grade Writers Learn about Themselves in the Midst of Others." *Voices from the Middle* 16.1 (2008): 9–14. Print. |
| Teaching writing and style | Butler, Paul. "Reconsidering the Teaching of Style." *English Journal* 100.4 (2011): 77–82. Print. |
| | Flynn, Jill Ewing. "The Language of Power: Beyond the Grammar Workbook." *English Journal* 100.4 (2011): 27–30. Print. |
| | Hillocks, George, Jr. *Teaching Argument Writing, Grades 6–12: Supporting Claims with Relevant Evidence and Clear Reasoning.* Portsmouth, NH: Heinemann, 2011. Print. |
| | Johnston, Jim. "A Joy to Teach: My Experience with a Student Writer." *Voices from the Middle* 18.3 (2011): 27–32. Print. |
| | Lain, Sheryl. "Reaffirming the Writing Workshop for Young Adolescents." *Voices from the Middle* 14.3 (2007): 20–28. Print. |
| | Wilde, Sandra. "'My Kids Can't Spell and I Don't Want to Deal with It': Spelling in Middle School." *Voices from the Middle* 15.3 (2008): 10–15. Print. |
| | Young, Art. "Writing Across and Against the Curriculum." *College Composition and Communication* 54.3 (2003): 472–85. Print. |
| Culturally and linguistically diverse students | Carter, Stephanie Power, James S. Damico, and Kafi Kumasi-Johnson. "The Time Is Now! Talking with African American Youth about College." *Voices from the Middle* 16.2 (2008): 47–53. Print. |
| | Fisher, Douglas, Carol Rothenberg, and Nancy Frey. *Language Learners in the English Classroom.* Urbana, IL: NCTE, 2007. Print. |
| | Kinloch, Valerie. *Harlem on Our Minds: Place, Race, and the Literacies of Urban Youth.* New York: Teachers College Press, 2010. Print. |
| | Redd, Teresa M., and Karen Schuster Webb. *A Teacher's Introduction to African American English: What a Writing Teacher Should Know.* Urbana, IL: NCTE, 2005. Print. |
| | Rodriguez, Eleanor Renée, and James Bellanca. *What Is It about Me That You Can't Teach? An Instructional Guide for the Urban Educator.* Thousand Oaks, CA: Corwin-Sage, 2007. Print. |
| | Souto-Manning, Mariana. "Teaching English Learners: Building on Cultural and Linguistic Strengths." *English Education* 42.3 (2010): 248–62. Print. |
| | Wickens, Corrine M., and Linda Wedwick. "Looking Forward: Increased Attention to LGBTQ Students and Families in Middle Grade Classrooms." *Voices from the Middle* 18.4 (2011): 43–51. Print. |

| Topic | Resource |
|-------|----------|
| Professional learning communities/ teacher communities | Cochran-Smith, Marilyn, and Susan L. Lytle. *Inquiry as Stance: Practitioner Research for the Next Generation.* New York: Teachers College Press, 2009. Print. |
| | Egawa, Kathryn A. "Good Talk about Good Teaching." *Voices from the Middle* 16.4 (2009): 9–16. Print. |
| | Fredrickson, James E. "Talking about Teaching: Establishing Trust amidst Uncertainty." *Voices from the Middle* 16.4 (2009): 38–40. Print. |
| | Seglem, Robyn. "Creating a Circle of Learning: Teachers Taking Ownership through Professional Communities." *Voices from the Middle* 16.4 (2009): 32–37. Print. |
| | Shanklin, Nancy. "Being Proactive about Your Professional Learning: What's the Payoff?" *Voices from the Middle* 16.4 (2009): 45–47. Print. |
| | Wirsing, Jan. "Regaining Momentum: Teacher Inquiry as Ongoing Professional Development." *Voices from the Middle* 16.4 (2009): 25–31. Print. |
| Communities outside of the classroom (family and peer influence) | Farrell, Albert D., David B. Henry, Sally A. Mays, and Michael E. Schoeny. "Parents as Moderators of the Impact of School Norms and Peer Influences on Aggression in Middle School Students." *Child Development* 82.1 (2011): 146–61. Print. |
| | Martínez, Rebecca S., O. Tolga Aricak, Misha N. Graves, Jessica Peters-Myszak, and Leah Nellis. "Changes in Perceived Social Support and Socioemotional Adjustment across the Elementary to Junior High School Transition." *Journal of Youth and Adolescents* 40.5 (2011): 519–30. Print. |
| Media literacy and technology in the classroom | Gainer, Jesse S. "Critical Media Literacy in Middle School: Exploring the Politics of Representation." *Journal of Adolescent and Adult Literacy* 53.5 (2010): 364–73. Print. |
| | Golden, John. *Reading in the Dark: Using Film as a Tool in the English Classroom.* Urbana, IL: NCTE, 2001. Print. |
| | Kajder, Sara. *Adolescents and Digital Literacies: Learning Alongside Our Students.* Urbana, IL: NCTE, 2010. Print. |
| | Labbo, Linda D., and Karen Place. "Fresh Perspectives on New Literacies and Technology Integration." *Voices from the Middle* 17.3 (2010): 9–18. Print. |
| | National Writing Project, Dánielle Nicole DeVoss, Elyse Eidman-Aadahl, and Troy Hicks. *Because Digital Writing Matters: Improving Student Writing in Online and Multimedia Environments.* San Francisco: Jossey-Bass, 2010. Print. |
| | Ranker, Jason. "The Interactive Potential of Multiple Media: A New Look at Inquiry Projects." *Voices from the Middle* 17.3 (2010): 36–43. Print. |
| | Skinner, Emily. "Writing Workshop Meets Critical Media Literacy: Using Magazines and Movies as Mentor Texts." *Voices from the Middle* 15.2 (2007): 30–39. Print. |
| | Stuart, Denise H. "Cin(E)-Poetry: Engaging the Digital Generation in 21st Century Response." *Voices from the Middle* 17.3 (2010): 27–35. Print. |
| Teaching literature and young adult literature | Campbell, Kimberly Hill. *Less Is More: Teaching Literature with Short Texts—Grades 6–12.* Portland, ME: Stenhouse, 2007. Print. |
| | Groenke, Susan L., Joellen Maples, and Jill Henderson. "Raising 'Hot Topics' through Young Adult Literature." *Voices from the Middle* 17.4 (2010): 29–36. Print. |
| | Hinton, KaaVonia, and Gail K. Dickinson. "Narrowing the Gap between Readers and Books." *Voices from the Middle* 13.1 (2005): 15–20. Print. |
| | Howard, Vivian. "The Importance of Pleasure Reading in the Lives of Young Teens: Self-Identification, Self-Construction and Self-Awareness." *Journal of Librarianship and Information Science* 43.1 (2011): 46–55. Print. |

| Topic | Resource |
|---|---|
| Teaching literature and young adult literature *(continued)* | Moen, Christine Boardman. "Bringing Words to Life and into the Lives of Middle School Students." *Voices from the Middle* 15.1 (2007): 20–26. Print. |
| | Smith, Michael W., and Jeffrey D. Wilhelm. *Fresh Takes on Teaching Literary Elements: How to Teach What Really Matters about Character, Setting, Point of View, and Theme.* New York: Scholastic; Urbana, IL: NCTE, 2010. Print. |
| Critical literacy | Heffernan, Lee, and Mitzi Lewison. "Keep Your Eyes on the Prize: Critical Stance in the Middle School Classroom." *Voices from the Middle* 17.2 (2009): 19–27. Print. |
| | Massey, Lance. "On the Richness of Grammar as an Analytical Lens in the Integrated Language Arts." *English Journal* 100.4 (2011): 66–70. Print. |
| | Patel Stevens, Lisa, and Thomas W. Bean. *Critical Literacy: Context, Research, and Practice in the K–12 Classroom.* Thousand Oaks, CA: Sage, 2007. Print. |
| | Shanklin, Nancy. "Using Critical Literacy to Engage Learners: What New Teachers Can Do." *Voices from the Middle* 17.2 (2009): 44–46. Print. |
| | White, John Wesley. "Reading 'the Word and the World': The Double-Edged Sword of Teaching Critical Literacy." *Voices from the Middle* 17.2 (2009): 55–57. Print. |
| | Wilson, Jennifer L., and Tasha Tropp Laman. "'That Was Basically Me': Critical Literacy, Text, and Talk." *Voices from the Middle* 15.2 (2007): 40–46. Print. |
| General advice/ direction for teachers | Meyer, Richard. "Future Directions: A Call for Actions." *Voices from the Middle* 18.4 (2011): 21–30. Print. |
| | Quate, Stevi, and John McDermott. *Clock Watchers: Six Steps to Motivating and Engaging Disengaged Students across Content Areas.* Portsmouth, NH: Heinemann, 2009. Print. |
| | Rose, Suzanne M. "'If Only It Weren't Such a Chore . . .': What Talented Eighth Graders Have to Say about Their ELA Classes." *Voices from the Middle* 18.3 (2011): 18–26. Print. |
| | Shanklin, Nancy. "Inventing Your Way into High-Quality Student Discussions." *Voices from the Middle* 18.2 (2010): 63–65. Print. |
| Standards and policy issues | Dolgin, Joanna, Kim Kelly, and Sarvenaz Zelkha. *Authentic Assessments for the English Classroom.* Urbana, IL: NCTE, 2010. Print. |
| | Newmann, Fred M., M. Bruce King, and Dana L. Carmichael. *Authentic Instruction and Assessment: Common Standards for Rigor and Relevance in Teaching Academic Subjects.* Des Moines: Iowa Department of Education, 2007. Print. |
| | Sipe, Rebecca Bowers. *Adolescent Literacy at Risk? The Impact of Standards.* Urbana, IL: NCTE, 2009. Print. |
| Instructional planning | Burke, Jim. *What's the Big Idea? Question-Driven Units to Motivate Reading, Writing, and Thinking.* Portsmouth, NH: Heinemann, 2010. Print. |

# Appendix B

*NCTE Principles*

Throughout this book, there have been references to the NCTE principles that guide inspiring and effective teachers such as those featured in the vignettes. Drawn from research and based on classroom practices that foster student learning, these principles provide the foundation on which excellent teaching and enhanced student learning is built. This section includes explanations of NCTE principles about several areas of instruction—reading, writing, speaking and listening, and language—along with principles on formative assessment, teaching English language learners, 21st century literacies, and the role of teachers as decision makers in planning and implementing instruction. This last is the overarching principle under which all the others are clustered because it speaks to the heart of teacher work.

The principles in this appendix represent a compilation of work created and endorsed by NCTE, much of which can be found and is referenced on the NCTE website. As you think about ways to begin planning and shifting your instruction to align with the CCSS, use this document as a reference and resource, grounding your instruction, as well, in established, research-based NCTE principles. Each set of principles is organized into two categories: what NCTE knows about learners and learning, and what that knowledge means for teachers in the classroom.

# NCTE Principles Regarding Teachers as Decision Makers

*A number of NCTE documents affirm the role of teachers as decision makers. Among the most recent are the 2005 "Features of Literacy Programs: A Decision-Making Matrix," produced by the Commission on Reading; the 2008 Resolution passed by the Board of Directors on Scripted Curricula; and the 2010 Resolution on Affirming the Role of Teachers and Students in Developing Curriculum.*

Both the CCSS and NCTE agree that teachers' professional judgment and experience should shape the way that the goals inherent in the CCSS will be reached. Common agreement on what students should be able to accomplish leaves ample room for teachers to make decisions about the materials and strategies that will be used in the classroom. Teachers are not simply implementation agents for the CCSS; rather, they are active shapers of schoolwide plans that will enable students to reach the goals of these or any standards.

The journeys recounted in this book demonstrate that teachers work, learn, and plan most effectively when they collaborate with their colleagues. Indeed, research shows that teaching teams are a vital unit of school change and improvement.

## What we know about teaching as a profession:

Working in teams allows teachers to design and share goals and strategies, strengthens the foundation for informed decision making, and contributes to participation in more broadly based communities of practice. Teaching teams bring together teachers, administrators, and other educators to:

- Develop and assess curricula
- Assess and become more knowledgeable about student learning
- Design and support activities that enhance professional practice
- Apply cross-disciplinary perspectives to curriculum design, assessment, and professional growth
- Conduct collective inquiry into the learning and teaching environment
- Connect to parents and the community

We also know that teaching is a professional endeavor, and that teachers are active problem solvers and decision makers in the classroom. As professionals, teachers and students benefit from sustained and empowering professional development for teachers.

## What this means for educators:

- Administrators and teacher leaders should provide for systematic professional development as an essential component of successful school reform. Teachers who have opportunities for quality professional development are best able to help students learn.

- We need to collectively define teacher effectiveness as professional practice that uses deep content knowledge, effective pedagogy, authentic formative assessments, connections with parents and communities, sustained reflection, and research-based practices to engage students and help them learn.

- Schools should support a comprehensive literacy policy as described in the Literacy Education for All, Results for the Nation (LEARN) Act that requires a sustained investment in literacy learning and instruction from birth through grade 12 and empowers teachers to design and select formative assessments and lessons.

# NCTE Principles Regarding Reading Instruction

*The original version of this NCTE Guideline, titled "On Reading, Learning to Read, and Effective Reading Instruction: An Overview of What We Know and How We Know It," can be found on NCTE's website at http://www.ncte.org/positions/statements/onreading and was authored by The Commission on Reading of the National Council of Teachers of English.*

As the teachers in this volume have demonstrated, reading instruction consumes a lot of our attention in the classroom. The creators of the CCSS have acknowledged the importance of literacy for twenty-first-century learners by including standards for literacy instruction across content areas; indeed, as reading materials become more diverse and complex in this digital age, we need to prepare our students to encounter different types of texts in different situations.

## What we know about reading and learning to read:

- Reading is a complex and purposeful sociocultural, cognitive, and linguistic process in which readers simultaneously use their knowledge of spoken and written language, their knowledge of the topic of the text, and their knowledge of their culture to construct meaning with text.

- Readers read for different purposes.

- As children learn to read continuous text, they use their intuitive knowledge of spoken language and their knowledge of the topic to figure out print words in text.

- The more children read, the better readers they become.

- Children read more when they have access to engaging, age-appropriate books, magazines, newspapers, computers, and other reading materials. They read more on topics that interest them than on topics that do not interest them.

- Reading supports writing development and writing supports reading development.

- All readers use their life experiences, their knowledge of the topic, and their knowledge of oral and written language to make sense of print.

- Readers continue to grow in their ability to make sense of an increasing variety of texts on an increasing variety of topics throughout their lives.

## What this means for teachers of reading:

- Teachers should know their students as individuals, including their interests, their attitudes about reading, and their school, home, and community experiences.

- Teachers should read to students daily using a variety of text types.

- Teachers should try to use a variety of instructional groupings, including whole-group, small-group, and individual instruction, to provide multiple learning experiences.
- Teachers should teach before-, during-, and after-reading strategies for constructing meaning of written language, including demonstrations and think-alouds.
- Teachers should provide specific feedback to students to support their reading development.
- Teachers should provide regular opportunities for students to respond to reading through discussion, writing, art, drama, storytelling, music, and other creative expressions.
- Teachers should provide regular opportunities for students to reflect on their learning.
- Teachers should gradually release instructional responsibility to support independent reading.
- Teachers need to reflect on their students' progress and their own teaching practices to make changes that meet the needs of students.

# NCTE Principles Regarding the Teaching of Writing

*The original version of this NCTE Guideline, titled "NCTE Beliefs about the Teaching of Writing," can be found on NCTE's website at http://www.ncte.org/positions/statements/writingbeliefs. It was originally authored by the Writing Study Group of the NCTE Executive Committee.*

Just as the nature of and expectation for literacy has changed in the past century and a half, so has the nature of writing. Much of that change has been due to technological developments, from pen and paper, to typewriter, to word processor, to networked computer, to design software capable of composing words, images, and sounds. These developments not only expanded the types of texts that writers produce, but they also expanded immediate access to a wider variety of readers. The CCSS acknowledge this reality with standards that note the need for students to be able to use technology critically and effectively in their writing, but it is up to teachers to decide how to engage students with meaningful writing tasks that will enable them to meet the demands of our quickly changing society.

## What we know about writing and learning to write:

- Everyone has the capacity to write, writing can be taught, and teachers can help students become better writers.
- People learn to write by writing.
- Writing is a process and a tool for thinking.
- Writing grows out of many different purposes.
- Conventions of finished and edited texts are important to readers and therefore to writers.
- Writing and reading are related.
- Literate practices are embedded in complicated social relationships.
- Composing occurs in different modalities and technologies.
- Assessment of writing involves complex, informed, human judgment.

# What this means for teachers of writing:

- Writing instruction must include ample in-class and out-of-class opportunities for writing and should include writing for a variety of purposes and audiences.
- Instruction should be geared toward making sense in a life outside of school.
- Writing instruction must provide opportunities for students to identify the processes that work best for themselves as they move from one writing situation to another.
- Writing instruction must take into account that a good deal of workplace writing and other writing takes place in collaborative situations.
- It is important that teachers create opportunities for students to be in different kinds of writing situations, where the relationships and agendas are varied.
- Simply completing workbook or online exercises is inadequate.
- Students should have access to and experience in reading material that presents both published and student writing in various genres.
- Students should be taught the features of different genres experientially, not only explicitly.
- The teaching of writing should assume students will begin with the sort of language with which they are most at home and most fluent in their speech.
- Writing instruction must accommodate the explosion in technology from the world around us.
- Instructors must recognize the difference between formative and summative evaluation and be prepared to evaluate students' writing from both perspectives.

# NCTE Principles Regarding
# Speaking and Listening

*NCTE principles on speaking and listening are articulated in "Guideline on the Essentials of English," which can be found at http://www.ncte.org/positions/statements/essentialsofenglish.*

NCTE has a long history of supporting both instruction and assessment that integrates speaking and listening skills into the teaching of the English language arts, and the CCSS acknowledge the importance of speaking and listening in their Speaking and Listening Standards. Speaking refers to both informal speech, such as talking in small groups or participating in class discussions, and formal speech that results from composing and presenting a text. Listening means engaging in a complex, active process that serves a variety of purposes.

## What we know about speaking and listening in school:

- Public speaking is consistently ranked as one of the greatest sources of anxiety for people of all ages, and students are no exception.
- Much of the work of the classroom is done through speaking and listening.
- Formal speaking can be extemporaneous, relying on detailed notes but no actual script, or text-based.
- If students spend discussion time competing for the attention of the teacher rather than listening and responding to peers, they will not benefit from the informal speech in the classroom.
- It can be difficult to evaluate listening.
- One of the advantages of speaking is that it can generate immediate response, and it is important to make full use of this feature.

## What this means for teachers of speaking and listening:

- To ensure that all students have an opportunity to develop skills of informal speech, teachers should not depend exclusively on volunteers in class discussion.
- Strategies for broadening participation include having all students respond in writing and then asking each student to respond aloud, asking students to discuss in pairs and report to the class, or distributing "talk tokens" that students can turn in after a contribution to a class discussion.

- Teachers should support the development of formal speaking and provide students with support and opportunities to practice so that they can feel well-prepared.
- Teachers need to give explicit attention to the connections between speaking and listening.
- To foster active listening, teachers can encourage students to build upon one another's contributions to discussions or require them to write a brief summary of the discussion at the end of class.

# NCTE Principles Regarding Language Instruction

*A comprehensive statement of NCTE's principles on language instruction appears in "Learning through Language: A Call for Action in All Disciplines," which can be found on NCTE's website at http://www.ncte.org/positions/statements/learningthroughlang. It was prepared by NCTE's Language and Learning across the Curriculum Committee.*

Language is a primary way individuals communicate what they think and feel. They find self-identity through language, shape their knowledge and experiences by means of it, and depend on it as a lifelong resource for expressing their hopes and feelings. One of the goals of language instruction is to foster language awareness among students so that they will understand how language varies in a range of social and cultural settings; how people's attitudes toward language vary across culture, class, gender, and generation; how oral and written language affects listeners and readers; how conventions in language use reflect social-political-economic values; how the structure of language works; and how first and second languages are acquired. The CCSS provide standards for language instruction, but teachers should use their knowledge of language to help foster an interest in language that is contextually bound to other literate practices.

## What we know about language and learning language:

- As human beings, we can put sentences together even as children—we can all do grammar.
- Students make errors in the process of learning, and as they learn about writing, they often make new errors, not necessarily fewer ones.
- Students benefit much more from learning a few grammar keys thoroughly than from trying to remember many terms and rules.
- Students find grammar most interesting when they apply it to authentic texts.
- Inexperienced writers find it difficult to make changes in the sentences that they have written.
- All native speakers of a language have more grammar in their heads than any grammar book will ever contain.

## What this means for teachers of language:

- Teachers should foster an understanding of grammar and usage.
- Instructors must integrate language study into all areas of the English language arts.
- Teachers should experiment with different approaches to language instruction until they find the ones that work the best for them and their students.
- Teachers should show students how to apply grammar not only to their writing but also to their reading and to their other language arts activities.
- Teachers can make good use of the other languages and the various dialects of English in their classrooms.
- Teachers might try using texts of different kinds, such as newspapers and the students' own writing, as sources for grammar examples and exercises.
- Teachers should use grammar exercises that improve writing, such as sentence combining and model sentences.

# NCTE Principles Regarding Teaching English Language Learners

*The original version of this NCTE Guideline, entitled "NCTE Position Paper on the Role of English Teachers in Educating English Language Learners (ELLs)," can be found on NCTE's website at http://www.ncte.org/positions/statements/teacherseducatingell. It was originally authored by members of the ELL Task Force: Maria Brisk, Stephen Cary, Ana Christina DaSilva Iddings, Yu Ren Dong, Kathy Escamilla, Maria Franquiz, David Freeman, Yvonne Freeman, Paul Kei Matsuda, Christina Ortmeier-Hooper, David Schwarzer, Katie Van Sluys, Randy Bomer (EC Liaison), and Shari Bradley (Staff Liaison).*

Multilingual students differ in various ways, including level of oral English proficiency, literacy ability in both the heritage language and English, and cultural background. English language learners born in the United States often develop conversational language abilities in English but lack academic language proficiency. Newcomers, on the other hand, need to develop both conversational and academic English. The creators of the CCSS note that the standards do not address the needs of English language learners (p. 6), but they also note that it is important for schools to consider and accommodate these students' needs while meeting the standards. These principles can provide a guide for teachers as they imagine what this might look like in their classrooms.

## What we know about teaching multilingual learners:

- The academic language that students need in the different content areas differs.
- English language learners need three types of knowledge to become literate in a second language: the second language, literacy, and world knowledge.
- Second language acquisition is a gradual developmental process and is built on students' knowledge and skill in their native language.
- Bilingual students also need to learn to read and write effectively to succeed in school.
- Writing well in English is often the most difficult skill for English language learners to master.
- English language learners may not be familiar with terminology and routines often associated with writing instruction in the United States, including writing process, drafting, revision, editing, workshop, conference, audience, purpose, or genre.

## What this means for teachers of multilingual students:

- For English language learners, teachers need to consider content objectives as well as English language development objectives.
- Because teachers relate to students both as learners and as children or adolescents, teachers must establish how they will address these two types of relationships, what they need to know about their students, and how they will acquire this knowledge.
- Teachers should provide authentic opportunities to use language in a nonthreatening environment.
- Teachers should encourage academic oral language in the various content areas.
- Teachers should give attention to the specific features of language students need to communicate in social as well as academic contexts.
- Teachers should include classroom reading materials that are culturally relevant.
- Teachers should ask families to read with students a version in the heritage language.
- Teachers should teach language features, such as text structure, vocabulary, and text- and sentence-level grammar, to facilitate comprehension of the text.
- Teachers should give students frequent meaningful opportunities for them to generate their own texts.
- Teachers should provide models of well-organized papers for the class.

# NCTE Principles Regarding
# 21st Century Literacies

*The original version of this Position Statement, titled "21st Century Curriculum and Assessment Framework," can be found on NCTE's website at http://www.ncte.org/positions/statements/21stcentframework. It was adopted by the NCTE executive committee on November 19, 2008.*

Literacy has always been a collection of cultural and communicative practices shared among members of particular groups. These literacies—from reading online newspapers to participating in virtual classrooms—are multiple, dynamic, and malleable. Students need to be able to navigate the multiple literacy situations in which they will find themselves, and undoubtedly, they already engage with a number of literacies that were not available to their parents and teachers. The CCSS include standards for students' effective and critical use of technology, and the following principles can help teachers consider how to implement instruction that will empower students as technology continues to change and affect their literacies.

## What we know about 21st century literacies and learning:

- As society and technology change, so does literacy.
- Because technology has increased the intensity and complexity of literate environments, the twenty-first century demands that a literate person possess a wide range of abilities and competencies, many literacies.
- Students in the twenty-first century need interpersonal skills to work collaboratively in both face-to-face and virtual environments to use and develop problem-solving skills.
- Students in the twenty-first century must be aware of the global nature of our world and be able to select, organize, and design information to be shared, understood, and distributed beyond their classrooms.
- Students in the twenty-first century must be able to take information from multiple places and in a variety of different formats, determine its reliability, and create new knowledge from that information.
- Students in the twenty-first century must be critical consumers and creators of multimedia texts.
- Students in the twenty-first century must understand and adhere to legal and ethical practices as they use resources and create information.

## What this means for teachers of twenty-first-century learners:

- Students should use technology as a tool for communication, research, and creation of new works.

- Students should find relevant and reliable sources that meet their needs.

- Teachers should encourage students to take risks and try new things with tools available to them.

- Teachers should create situations and assignments in which students work in a group in ways that allow them to create new knowledge or to solve problems that can't be created or solved individually.

- Students should work in groups of members with diverse perspectives and areas of expertise.

- Students should be given opportunities to share and publish their work in a variety of ways.

- Teachers should help students analyze the credibility of information and its appropriateness in meeting their needs.

- Students should have the tools to critically evaluate their own and others' multimedia works.

# NCTE Principles Regarding Assessment

*The original version of this document, titled "Standards for the Assessment of Reading and Writing, Revised Edition (2009)," can be found on NCTE's website at http://www.ncte.org/standards/assessmentstandards. This document was authored by members of the Joint IRA–NCTE Task Force on Assessment, Peter Johnston (chair), Peter Afflerbach, Sandra Krist, Kathryn Mitchell Pierce, Elizabeth Spalding, Alfred W. Tatum, and Sheila W. Valencia.*

Assessment is an integral part of instruction, and NCTE affirms its importance for student learning. In particular, formative assessment can be a powerful means of improving student achievement because it is assessment *for* learning, but it must adhere to key principles to be effective. These principles include emphasizing timely and task-focused feedback because it is feedback, not the absence of a grade, that characterizes effective formative assessment; shaping instructional decisions based on student performance in formative assessment; embedding formative assessment in instruction because the use of a given instrument of assessment, not the instrument itself, confers value on formative assessment; and offering students increased opportunities to understand their own learning. The principles below, developed in collaboration with the International Reading Association, suggest how assessment, both formative and summative, can enhance student achievement.

## What we know about assessment:

- Assessment experiences at all levels, whether formative or summative, have consequences for students.

- Assessment should emphasize what students can do rather than what they cannot do.

- Assessment must provide useful information to inform and enable reflection.

- If any individual student's interests are not served by an assessment practice, regardless of whether it is intended for administration or decision making by an individual or by a group, then that practice is not valid for that student.

- The most productive and powerful assessments for students are likely to be the formative assessments that occur in the daily activities of the classroom.

- The teacher is the most important agent of assessment.

- Teachers need to feel safe to share, discuss, and critique their own work with others.

- Teacher knowledge cannot be replaced by standardized tests.

- The primary purpose of assessment is to improve teaching and learning.

## What this means for teachers:

- Teachers should be able to demonstrate how their assessment practices benefit and do not harm individual students.
- Teachers must be aware of and deliberate about their roles as assessors.
- Teachers must have routines for systematic assessment to ensure that each student is benefiting optimally from instruction.
- Teacher leaders and administrators need to recognize that improving teachers' assessment expertise requires ongoing professional development, coaching, and access to professional learning communities. Nurturing such communities must be a priority for improving assessment.
- Teachers must take responsibility for making and sharing judgments about students' achievements and progress.
- Teachers should give students multiple opportunities to talk about their writing.
- Schools and teachers must develop a trusting relationship with the surrounding community.

# Author

Tonya Perry is an assistant professor of English education in the School of Education at the University of Alabama at Birmingham. Her work is primarily in literacy practices for diverse middle school students and urban education. As a director and principal investigator for the National Writing Project's UAB Red

Mountain Writing Project site, Perry works with teachers across multiple school districts to impact literacy skills. Her interest in the Common Core State Standards arose from teachers' desire to know more about them and how to transition their teaching to meet the new demands. As a classroom teacher for ten years and teacher educator for eleven, Perry has learned the importance of quality professional development, in its many forms, for influencing student learning. She was also a national finalist for Teacher of the Year in 2001.

# Contributing Author

As a professional development specialist for the Chicago Teachers' Center of Northeastern Illinois University from 1996 to 2010, **Rebecca Manery** provided instructional support in literacy to hundreds of teachers and students in dozens of Chicago public elementary and high schools. The coauthor of a high school transition literacy curriculum and a college essay writing curriculum for students at twenty-one GEAR UP high schools, she also cofounded the Teachers as Writers professional development program, codirected CTC's Young Adult Literature Conference, and served as an adjunct instructor in NEIU's graduate program in Reading. Manery is currently pursuing doctoral studies in the Joint Program in English and Education at the University of Michigan.

This book was typeset in TheMix and Palatino by Precision Graphics.

The typeface used on the cover is Myriad Pro.

The book was printed on 60-lb. White Recycled Opaque Offset paper by Versa Press, Inc.

*30% Total Recycled Fiber*

## DATE DUE

PRINTED IN U.S.A.